A Retreat With Therese of Lisieux

Other titles in the
A Retreat With... *Series:*

A RETREAT WITH THERESE OF LISIEUX

Loving Our Way Into Holiness

Elizabeth Ruth Obbard, O.D.C.

ST. ANTHONY MESSENGER PRESS

Cincinnati, Ohio

Scripture citations are taken from the *New Revised Standard Version Bible*, copyright ©1989 by the Division of Christian Education of the National Council of Churches of Christ in the U.S.A. and used by permission.

Excerpts from *The Autobiography of Therese of Lisieux*, translated by Ronald Knox, translated by Ronald Knox, copyright ©1958 by P.J. Kenedy & Sons, are reprinted with permission of the publisher.

Excerpts from *A Memoir of My Sister*, by Sister Genevieve of the Holy Face, translated by Ronald Knox, copyright ©1958 by P.J. Kenedy & Sons, are reprinted with permission of the publisher.

Excerpts of *The Collected Letters of St. Therese of Lisieux*, translated by F.J. Sheed, copyright ©1949 by Sheed & Ward, are reprinted with permission of the publisher.

Cover illustration by Steve Erspamer, S.M.
Cover and book design by Mary Alfieri

ISBN 0-86716-242-2

Copyright ©1996, Elizabeth Ruth Obbard

Published by St. Anthony Messenger Press
Printed in the U.S.A.

FOR MY FAMILY—
so different from Therese's family
but so dear to me:
   my parents, Robert and Rhoda,
   my brother and sister, Bob and Jean,
   and their children:
      Howard, Thomas, Caroline,
      Rebecca, Katherine, David

Acknowledgments

I am especially grateful to Sister Margaret Needham for typing the manuscript and for giving me her own translation of Therese's "Letter to Marie," which forms the central part of the saint's autobiography, and her "Offering to Merciful Love."

Contents

Introducing A Retreat With...

Twenty years ago I made a weekend retreat at a Franciscan house on the coast of New Hampshire. The retreat director's opening talk was as lively as a long-range weather forecast. He told us how completely God loves each one of us—without benefit of lively anecdotes or fresh insights.

As the friar rambled on, my inner critic kept up a sotto voce commentary: "I've heard all this before." "Wish he'd say something new that I could chew on." "That poor man really doesn't have much to say." Ever hungry for manna yet untasted, I devalued any experience of hearing the same old thing.

After a good night's sleep, I awoke feeling as peaceful as a traveler who has at last arrived safely home. I walked across the room toward the closet. On the way I passed the sink with its small framed mirror on the wall above. Something caught my eye like an unexpected presence. I turned, saw the reflection in the mirror and said aloud, "No wonder he loves me!"

This involuntary affirmation stunned me. What or whom had I seen in the mirror? When I looked again, it was "just me," an ordinary person with a lower-than-average reservoir of self-esteem. But I knew that in the initial vision I had seen God-in-me breaking through like a sudden sunrise.

At that moment I knew what it meant to be made in the divine image. I understood right down to my size eleven feet what it meant to be loved exactly as I was.

Only later did I connect this revelation with one granted to the Trappist monk-writer Thomas Merton. As he reports in *Conjectures of a Guilty Bystander*, while standing all unsuspecting on a street corner one day, he was overwhelmed by the "joy of being...a member of a race in which God Himself became incarnate.... There is no way of telling people that they are all walking around shining like the sun."

As an absentminded homemaker may leave a wedding ring on the kitchen windowsill, so I have often mislaid this precious conviction. But I have never forgotten that particular retreat. It persuaded me that the Spirit rushes in where it will. Not even a boring director or a judgmental retreatant can withstand the "violent wind" that "fills the entire house" where we dwell in expectation (see Acts 2:2).

So why deny ourselves any opportunity to come aside awhile and rest on holy ground? Why not withdraw from the daily web that keeps us muddled and wound? Wordsworth's complaint is ours as well: "The world is too much with us." There is no flu shot to protect us from infection by the skepticism of the media, the greed of commerce, the alienating influence of technology. We need retreats as the deer needs the running stream.

An Invitation

This book and its companions in the *A Retreat With...* series from St. Anthony Messenger Press are designed to meet that need. They are an invitation to choose as director some of the most powerful, appealing and wise mentors our faith tradition has to offer.

Our directors come from many countries, historical eras and schools of spirituality. At times they are teamed

2

to sing in close harmony (for example, Francis de Sales, Jane de Chantal and Aelred of Rievaulx on spiritual friendship). Others are paired to kindle an illuminating fire from the friction of their differing views (such as Augustine of Hippo and Mary Magdalene on human sexuality). All have been chosen because, in their humanness and their holiness, they can help us grow in self-knowledge, discernment of God's will and maturity in the Spirit.

Inviting us into relationship with these saints and holy ones are inspired authors from today's world, women and men whose creative gifts open our windows to the Spirit's flow. As a motto for the authors of our series, we have borrowed the advice of Dom Frederick Dunne to the young Thomas Merton. Upon joining the Trappist monks, Merton wanted to sacrifice his writing activities lest they interfere with his contemplative vocation. Dom Frederick wisely advised, "Keep on writing books that make people love the spiritual life."

That is our motto. Our purpose is to foster (or strengthen) friendships between readers and retreat directors—friendships that feed the soul with wisdom, past and present. Like the scribe "trained for the kingdom of heaven," each author brings forth from his or her storeroom "what is new and what is old" (Matthew 13:52).

The Format

The pattern for each *A Retreat With...* remains the same; readers of one will be in familiar territory when they move on to the next. Each book is organized as a seven-session retreat that readers may adapt to their own schedules or to the needs of a group.

Day One begins with an anecdotal introduction called "Getting to Know Our Director(s)." Readers are given a telling glimpse of the guide(s) with whom they will be sharing the retreat experience. A second section, "Placing Our Director(s) in Context," will enable retreatants to see the guides in their own historical, geographical, cultural and spiritual settings.

Having made the human link between seeker and guide, the authors go on to "Introducing Our Retreat Theme." This section clarifies how the guide(s) are especially suited to explore the theme and how the retreatant's spirituality can be nourished by it.

After an original "Opening Prayer" to breathe life into the day's reflection, the author, speaking with and through the mentor(s), will begin to spin out the theme. While focusing on the guide(s)' own words and experience, the author may also draw on Scripture, tradition, literature, art, music, psychology or contemporary events to illuminate the path.

Each day's session is followed by reflection questions designed to challenge, affirm and guide the reader in integrating the theme into daily life. A "Closing Prayer" brings the session full circle and provides a spark of inspiration for the reader to harbor until the next session.

Days Two through Six begin with "Coming Together in the Spirit" and follow a format similar to Day One. Day Seven weaves the entire retreat together, encourages a continuation of the mentoring relationship and concludes with "Deepening Your Acquaintance," an envoi to live the theme by God's grace, the director(s)' guidance and the retreatant's discernment. A closing section of Resources serves as a larder from which readers may draw enriching books, videos, cassettes and films.

We hope readers will experience at least one of those memorable "No wonder God loves me!" moments. And we hope that they will have "talked back" to the mentor(s), as good friends are wont to do.

A case in point: There was once a famous preacher who always drew a capacity crowd to the cathedral. Whenever he spoke, an eccentric old woman sat in the front pew directly beneath the pulpit. She took every opportunity to mumble complaints and contradictions— just loud enough for the preacher to catch the drift that he was not as wonderful as he was reputed to be. Others seated down front glowered at the woman and tried to shush her. But she went right on needling the preacher to her heart's content.

When the old woman died, the congregation was astounded at the depth and sincerity of the preacher's grief. Asked why he was so bereft, he responded, "Now who will help me to grow?"

All of our mentors in *A Retreat With...* are worthy guides. Yet none would seek retreatants who simply said, "Where you lead, I will follow. You're the expert." In truth, our directors provide only half the retreat's content. Readers themselves will generate the other half.

As general editor for the retreat series, I pray that readers will, by their questions, comments, doubts and decision-making, fertilize the seeds our mentors have planted.

And may the Spirit of God rush in to give the growth.

Gloria Hutchinson
Series Editor
Conversion of Saint Paul, 1995

Getting to Know Our Director

Few, if any, saints have left behind so many photographs as Therese Martin, the popular saint of Lisieux. Looking through her photo album we can see her throughout her life's journey.

Here she is as a pouting three-year-old, with her hand on a chair back. It is clear that she already has a mind of her own.

Here she is at eight with her sister Celine, a child in a stiff pleated dress, tight jacket and buttoned boots. She holds a jump rope but doesn't look as if she played with it much. Her hair is in long fair ringlets with curly bangs across the forehead.

Here she is at thirteen, a pleasant open-faced girl, gazing thoughtfully into the future like any adolescent. At fifteen with her hair up in a modish chignon, she is prepared to impress the bishop with her uncommon maturity.

There follows a whole range of photographs in her chosen life as a Carmelite nun, most of them taken by her sister Celine, who had her own camera: Therese with the novices; Therese posing with her three Carmelite sisters and her cousin; Therese acting the part of Joan of Arc in a play she has written (casting herself in the starring role); Therese with the community making hay, helping with the wash, standing at a table as sacristan, holding an hourglass. We do not have to look hard at these photos to pick out her face in a group—the strong jaw and firm mouth, the clear, candid eyes, the relatively tall stature for a woman of her day.

Then there are pictures of Therese alone, her eyes showing the dark circles of encroaching sickness, others that show her emaciated form lying on an improvised bed in the fresh air.

In most of the photos, Therese looks like any other child of her time and culture, doing what her companions are doing, an ordinary Victorian girl next door. Yet this is the woman who has been called the greatest saint of modern times. Who is she and in what does her holiness consist? Above all, how can she share with us today the secret she discovered—that holiness is within the grasp of all?

Nothing about Therese's childhood would make us suspect her future sanctity. She was born on January 2, 1873, in Alençon, Normandy, to Louis and Zelie Martin, the youngest of their nine children, of whom five girls survived: Marie, Pauline, Leonie, Celine and Therese. As so often happens, the two oldest and the two youngest became close confidantes, while the middle one, Leonie, seemed "left out," "different" and was in fact the only sister who did not, in due course, enter the same convent as the other four.

Zelie Martin was the most powerful influence in this middle-class family—an overworked wife who ran a lacemaking business from her home, whose husband had given up his trade of watchmaker in mid-life. Zelie doted on her children, dressing them up and showing them off with pride (except for poor Leonie, who had no knack of fitting into the family pattern of the "good child"). Therese, the last born, was welcomed joyfully and petted often. All her earliest memories, she said, were of smiles and caresses, although she was not spoiled by anyone except her doting father.

But already Zelie was showing signs of the breast

cancer that would ultimately kill her. She could not feed the infant and Therese had to be sent out to a wet nurse. For four idyllic years—until Zelie's death—Therese developed as a confident and loving child.

Looking back, she remembered an incident which she felt summed up her whole attitude to life. She and Celine were playing in the garden when Leonie came along with a basket of doll clothes, ribbons, laces and pieces of fabric. On top sat her doll. Leonie had decided that she was too old for such playthings, so she told her little sisters to take their pick from the basket. Celine politely chose a ball of colored thread. Therese pondered, then suddenly said, "I choose the whole lot," and marched off with everything that was left.

That was to become the hallmark of her sanctity: "I choose everything." I choose all that God has chosen to offer. I don't want to be a saint by halves. I want everything, and I put out my hands to grasp this gift in its fullness. This early attitude Therese was to refind and refine many times.

After her mother's death in 1877, the four-year-old child was devastated. The house at Alençon was sold and the Martins moved to Lisieux to be near Zelie's brother and his family. Louis became a semirecluse, living only for his daughters and the practice of his religion. He doted on Therese. She was his "little queen"; he filled her world and became her primary focus. Pauline was appointed Therese's "second Mama," but no one could really take Zelie's place.

Her mother's death transformed Therese into an introverted, hypersensitive little girl, fearful of "outsiders." Within the family circle she could relax and be happy, but her former carefree temperament became scrupulous. She found refuge and security only in religious practices and a growing attraction to prayer.

She was what the people of Lisieux termed a shy, nervous child.

For a short while Therese attended a school conducted by local Benedictine nuns. It was an unhappy experience. Children of her own age, with their competitive games and petty rivalries, bewildered her. Then, to her anguish, Pauline left home to become a nun and Therese lost her "second Mama." This loss triggered what can only be termed a severe nervous breakdown.

Therese developed alarming psychosomatic symptoms: violent shivering, contortions, hallucinations. For two months her sanity and even her life were in doubt. But already, beneath the surface, there were signs that this weepy, hypersensitive girl was developing secret strength. She struggled to overcome her tears. She really wanted to please God. She wanted to be true to the demands of conscience whatever the cost. Her First Communion was a day of grace, of personal encounter with Jesus. She resolved to give herself completely to him—but what a wretched, weak person she felt herself to be!

As her fourteenth birthday approached, the thought of religious life that she had harbored for a long time received fresh impetus. She wanted to join her sisters Marie and Pauline in the Lisieux Carmel, but she was only fourteen. People judged her far too young to embrace such a life-style. But Louis gave his consent, and she decided to fight for the necessary permissions, going to the convent's superior, then the bishop. When the bishop hesitated, Therese, together with Louis and her inseparable sister Celine, joined a pilgrimage to Rome, determined to ask the pope himself to grant her request.

It was an eye-opening experience for this provincial girl, including as it did, a European tour which culminated in a papal audience for the pilgrims. Celine and Therese stood in line with the other women, black mantillas covering their fair hair. Suddenly Therese felt herself losing her nerve. It was announced that those being presented were not to speak to the Holy Father—and she had always been obedient! She quailed as she approached Leo XIII's throne.

"Speak," urged Celine the Intrepid (her family nickname), giving Therese a prod. Therese gathered all her courage and begged the pope to let her enter Carmel at fifteen. She was so distraught that she reiterated her request, clasping his knees, while her tears fell in a shower and the papal attendants looked on with disapproval at this display of emotion.

The pope advised Therese to do whatever her superiors told her. But that was not enough for the girl who chose everything. She insisted, as the attendants were loosening her grasp of the pontiff's knees, "Yes, but if you'd say the word, Most Holy Father, everybody would agree." Leo XIII must have smiled at her devout obstinacy as he replied, "All's well, all's well; if God wants you to enter, you will."

Poor Therese—all that effort and nothing to show for it! She returned to Lisieux disappointed. But her courage had been noticed. After Christmas the necessary permission arrived from the bishop. The way ahead was open.

So at fifteen, all obstacles overcome, Therese stood at the door of the Carmel on April 9, 1888, ready to embark on the life of her choice. Her fair hair was piled up on her head and she wore a fashionable blue costume—a typical teenager. All around her the family wept, but she remained calm, determined and resolute. Her childhood was over. She was set on becoming a saint.

The order Therese chose was that of the Carmelites as reformed by Saint Teresa of Avila in the sixteenth century. A nun's day in Carmel was a fine balance between solitude, work and community acts, all in the service of a life of perpetual prayer. Two hours daily were devoted to personal prayer, in addition to the full Divine Office (Liturgy of the Hours) and other religious practices. Life was simple, more like a family than a large monastic community (Carmels were limited to twenty-one nuns). The emphasis was on poverty, silence, enclosure—"a desert within the city." Therese embarked enthusiastically on the regime. It was what she wanted. This would be her contribution to the Church of her time; through prayer she would give souls to the Lord.

But how would this cosseted girl, so piously reared and so sheltered, survive the desert? She plunged into it and discovered aspects of herself she did not even know existed—an ability to endure, to accept herself with disconcerting truthfulness. The key was love and confidence; love of God and others, fidelity to conscience, a relentless search for truth in the Scriptures—especially the words of Jesus—and confidence in his mercy and power.

The setting was so ordinary that we can all identify with Therese as she struggled to find and become her better self. She wrestled, as we all must, with her own defects of character, the necessity of forming and sustaining relationships with those for whom she felt little sympathy, the requirements of extended prayer time when the Lord seemed absent; cold weather, unpalatable food, daily labor. But there were also times of celebration, happy moments of conversation and affection, shared tasks and ideals—the stuff of most lives.

A trial from which she suffered unspeakably was the breakdown of her adored father shortly after she entered the convent. For some time previously his mental and physical powers had seemed to fail, but there was no cause for real concern. It is possible that the loss of his youngest and favorite daughter was the final blow that unhinged his mind. In those days there was little understanding of or sympathy for mental illness. Louis Martin suffered loss of memory, urges to wander, occasional violent reactions—all symptoms that today might be assigned to Alzheimer's disease. He was present when Therese received the habit, "his last triumph" as she put it; the following month he was in an institution in Caen run by the Sisters of Bon Sauveur. The whole family was distressed and humiliated by his fate. Only when paralysis had set in and Louis could no longer be considered a danger to himself or others was he allowed home, where Leonie and Celine cared for him until his death.

Toward the end of her life, Therese herself faced a period of great darkness when it seemed to her that she had lost her faith. She tasted for the first time what many experience, the absence of God—coupled for her with the ravages of tuberculosis and conflicting emotions about her approaching death.

At twenty-four Therese was dying. On Holy Thursday (March 1896) she began hemorrhaging blood from her lungs. Although she reported this to Mother Marie de Gonzague, Therese asked for no special treatment and received none. The tuberculosis quickly advanced. Therese suffered nightly coughing fits, fevers, exhaustion. Her superior, who apparently saw this as an opportunity to act "for the good of Therese's soul," refused to provide morphine. Thoughts of suicide and annihilation passed through the patient's fevered brain. "I only suffer," she said, "minute after minute." God seemed to have forgotten her.

Yet this young woman who had led so ordinary a life was soon recognized as a saint. In her bewilderment and seeming failure she had struggled to love, to live up to her initial vision. She had tried to respond faithfully to the Lord of her heart, to follow the gospel. She had clung in blind trust and triumphed.

As she matured, slowly and painfully, Therese discovered the core of the Good News. She had not chosen God (though at first it had seemed so); God had chosen her. Not because of her youth and ardor, her pious upbringing and faithful observance of the Carmelite Rule, not for her strength of will or her heroic life: God had chosen her purely out of love, and she had responded with the confidence of a child. God had been merciful towards someone weak and imperfect and needy. It was all gift, all grace.

Here was the discovery—rediscovery—of a way open to anyone who wanted sanctity. Holiness was love: God loving us first and seeking our response. If God could make Therese a saint, then there was hope for everyone who desired sanctity as she did. The way is simple: the path of complete trust, a child's trust in a loving Parent. She called her path the "little way" and anchored it in the word of God.

Simple but not easy, the "little way" challenges our notions of sanctity as personal achievement, as strength of character, as undeviating fulfillment of laws and rules. It roots us in the sanctity of reality—the here and now, in ordinary life, lived under the providence of God.

Toward the end of her life Therese wrote: *"If only all the weak and imperfect people in the world could feel as I do [about the love and mercy of God], there'd be no reason why a single one should despair of scaling the hill of love and reaching the very top. Our Lord does not ask for great achievements, only for self-surrender and for gratitude."*[1]

In her dying months Therese knew with a deep, inarticulate certainty that she had attained sanctity because she had been loved and had loved in return. She had trusted in God and had not been disappointed. And the way she had followed was open to all who were willing to enter upon it.

Unlike more traditional methods of spiritual formation which required numerous acts of recognizable virtue, Therese's way requires only one thing. *"My director, Jesus, does not teach me to count my acts, but to do everything for love...but all this in peace, in abandonment. Jesus does everything, I nothing."*[2]

Placing Our Director In Context

Born toward the end of the nineteenth century, Therese entered the world when middle-class religion in France was narrow and rule-bound. The French Revolution toppled the Church in France from its position of power. *Liberty, equality* and *fraternity*, the watchwords of the new secular society, were held suspect by religious people, who tended to distance themselves from politics and the wider culture.

Therese's family was part of the rising bourgeoisie, secure, self-satisfied and self-contained, with little interest in anything outside their own social and religious sphere. The Martins were influenced by Jansenism, a seventeenth-century theology focused on predestination, a pessimistic view of humanity and rigorous moral principles. Their sights were set on heaven; the world was filled with temptations to be avoided on the way to the final goal.

A comparison might be drawn with some of the immigrant communities of the same time in the United States, who nurtured their own religious and cultural life apart from "outsiders." They kept to themselves and their own time-honored customs in order to protect their children from influences they considered dangerous and undesirable. The benefits of a democratic society were revered even while its philosophy was held slightly suspect.

Therese was nurtured in this kind of milieu, with all its limitations. Her parents were comfortably off, thanks to their own industry, and she had the benefit of a middle-class home with its relative comfort.

But life was far from ideal. She was the youngest child of a working mother and later of a one-parent family, with all the attendant difficulties and challenges. She had gone through a period of neurosis in girlhood, and her father suffered from a humiliating mental illness. After the loss of her mother, Therese was fearful, timid and self-protective. She grew up in a Church that stressed authority and fostered fear of the body, fear of free expression, fear of feelings.

There was a tendency to identify religion with good manners, financial comfort, exterior conformity. The outward stamp of religion was put on everything, just as in the United States, where a grade-school text series offered a separate edition for children in Catholic schools, in which science, for example, was taught by a mythical "Sister Anne." It was as if "Sister Anne" somehow made scientific experiments more "holy" than those conducted by plain Miss Smith in the public school.

In such an atmosphere the life of a priest or nun tended to be overvalued and marriage considered only second-best. Both Zelie and Louis Martin had been frustrated in their desire for religious vocations. When they were first wed, Louis announced that theirs would be a "Josephite Marriage" (without sexual intercourse). A year later, however, their first child was born. Neither Therese nor any of her sisters regarded marriage as a desirable option. It is therefore all the more surprising to find that Therese speaks as powerfully to the married as to the single person of our day.

Carmel, the order Therese entered, was also limited in the kind of women it attracted and kind of work they did. Behind the walls of the convent, Therese lived an uneventful, domestic life. She taught no pupils, nursed no sick poor, did not engage in a missionary apostolate (much as she was attracted to the missions). She did not even do the hard, dirty work that might have come the way of a Sister of Charity. Yet in and through her life situation, with all its limitations, Therese found a way to holiness that was full of confidence and love; her way was devoid of all fear and timidity in approaching God.

Therese, naturally good as she was, knew intuitively that goodness is not holiness. Holiness is not something we can attain by our own efforts. Holiness is God touching and transforming even the most ordinary life. We need only the boldness to claim this gift, the boldness of a child who trusts absolutely in a parent's love and generosity.

Therese read the Gospels assiduously and thus saw past the God of merit and reward to the God of unconditional love. In the Gospels she discovered a God who loves the weak and imperfect, the sinners and prostitutes, the lepers and tax collectors.

Therese's life was made up of common tasks, daily responsibilities of a small kind, household chores and community commitments. Like us, she experienced the joys of family life as well as the heartbreaks to which all intimate relationships expose us. By her very ordinariness, Therese reaches out to people in all walks of life.

Even someone like Dorothy Day, so deeply involved in alleviating suffering and in social action, found in

Therese real inspiration despite the two women's outwardly different life-circumstances. Dorothy, cofounder of the Catholic Worker Movement, named her daughter Tamar Teresa after our saint and wrote a book on Therese's life. For Dorothy saw that, however politically or socially involved a person may be, the love that motivates him or her is far more important than exterior accomplishments.

Therese managed to convert all the events of her life, great and small, into love—and only love counts in the end. She had a Midas touch. Everything was a treasure given by God; in touching it she discovered the hidden gold. She revealed a way to holiness that is within the reach of all.

Despite her cultural poverty and narrow religious upbringing Therese blazed a trail, cutting across all self-righteousness and smugness to center herself on a God of compassion who welcomes sinners and "little ones." Therese's teaching has so entered into the mainstream of Catholic consciousness that we now take it for granted.

After her death, when her sisters arranged for Therese's writings to be printed, what she had to say literally took the world by storm. Here was an ordinary young woman who had attained sanctity by a path all could recognize and claim as their own. People loved her, not merely admired her. Beneath the plush, bourgeois exterior, the sentimental language, the roses and lace, beat a heart authentic, faithful and bold.

Therese was recognized and acclaimed by the thousands who read her autobiography and clamored for her canonization. Theologians expounded her doctrine, popes lauded her, her influence has been quite unparalleled in modern times. Yet at fifteen she had hidden herself away in a convent and was known to very few outside her own family.

What did she really have to say? Is her message for today as it was for the men and women of yesterday? Yes, because it is pure gospel teaching, perennially valid, ancient yet ever new.

Holiness is God's gift. If we want this gift, we can have it. It is as simple as that. We have only to give ourselves to the particular life God has given us, and to do so with love. As Therese wrote, "It's love I ask for, love is all the skill I need."

Notes

1 "Letter to Marie."

2 "Letter CXXI," July 6, 1893, from *Collected Letters of St. Therese of Lisieux*, ed. Abbe Combes, trans. F. J. Sheed. New York: Sheed & Ward, 1949.

DAY ONE
You Are Loved

Introducing Our Retreat Theme

The theme of our retreat is loving our way into holiness—a holiness that is accessible to all of us, whatever our state in life, our natural gifts or limitations. God invites each of us to share as fully as possible in the divine life. We cannot earn holiness any more than we can earn love.

Holiness, therefore, is not a matter of multiplying religious practices. It is rather a way of living that allows God to take possession of our hearts and transform us into loving, Christlike women and men. Holiness is not about attainments but about letting go, about receiving the gift God wants to give by holding out empty hands for God to fill.

These insights on holiness did not come to Therese overnight. When she said she wanted to be a saint, to "choose all," go the whole way, others thought her presumptuous and told her so. Who was she to aim so high? She was a nobody, a barely educated young woman who couldn't even keep the convent rules perfectly. She did nothing outstanding. Indeed, she was not particularly good at her ordinary work. She ate normal meals instead of fasting and did no extra penances.

In Therese's time people tended toward the opinion

that holiness was way beyond the reach of most Christians, an unattainable goal. They thought holiness had to do with being extraordinary in some way, possessing unusual psychic gifts, enjoying mystical experiences, praying for long hours, never losing one's calm exterior, holding oneself aloof from the world and secular life.

Therese at first accepted this outlook unquestioningly. But she was a sharp observer of others and came to her own conclusions as she matured. People could be pursuing what they considered holiness and still be unloving, unfree, childish, unkind and un-Christlike. So how could they be holy?

Therese realized that these people had made themselves like the Pharisees in the Gospels. They thought themselves above others who were less gifted, less mortified. Their spiritual and psychic gifts had become riches, possessions that held them back from running to God with empty hands, trusting in God and not in themselves.

Such people think they have it made, that they are not like others. They consider themselves not sinners but mortified, detached religious folk who keep all the rules. Maybe they are, but that is not holiness.

Holiness is God's work. We can only come to God as we are: weak, needy, poor, without pretensions. Yet we must come with great confidence that we are loved and that God wants to share divine love and life with us. For that, we don't need extraordinary gifts. We don't have to be perfect, only "on the way." As Therese says, *All one has to do is to love Jesus, not considering oneself, not examining one's faults too closely.*[1]

Who is the person who does not desire with all her heart to possess the virtues? This longing is common to everyone. On the other hand, how very few there are in the spiritual life who are willing to fail, to stumble and fall, to be happy when others find them prostrate on the ground?[2]

Therese was not interested in success, she was interested only in the "science of love" that would lead her to true holiness, for only love makes us what God wants us to be. The rest is worthless.

Towards the end of her life Therese, looking back, wrote the story of her life, which she saw as the story of God's love and mercy towards her.

She reflected on her childhood and girlhood with its growing pains, its joys and sorrows. She reflected on her life as a nun, outwardly uneventful, yet a time when she learned from experience what it meant to love Jesus in day-to-day living. She wrote a long letter to her sister Marie, describing the path she had taken to holiness, a path of love, trust and utter confidence in God's mercy. Her autobiography, *The Story of a Soul*, was the fruit of years of reflection, when she had attained inner peace.

But Therese wrote numerous other letters that show her struggling in the midst of her trials. They reveal the anguish and desolation she felt at the time of her father's illness, her own loneliness, the painful choices she had to make in relationships, her lack of human support and understanding despite the presence of loving sisters.

Therese was later given the job of teaching and guiding the novices of the convent, young women taking their first steps in religious life. With them she shared her insights, helping them to deepen their relationship with Jesus and with one another. To them she showed the "way of spiritual childhood" that she had developed, and from her talks to the novices Celine Martin compiled a book of reminiscences.

Pauline Martin also kept a record of Therese's words during the months in which she lay dying, feeling that God had deserted her, her young body riddled with tuberculosis, her intestines causing her acute pain.

Our retreat will draw on all this material but will focus especially on Therese's letter to Marie, which encapsulates Therese's "little way," and also the text of an offering of herself to the merciful love of God that she made two years before her death.

Therese is uniquely able to help us because most of us, like her, live rather uneventful lives, made up of numerous small challenges. She shows us how to make our daily life itself the material of spiritual growth, wholeness and holiness. She shows us how to suffuse life with love. We know, for she tells us in her writings, that she followed her insights relentlessly, fearlessly. Her "way of spiritual childhood" is the fruit of her experience and she wishes to share it with us.

In this retreat she will be a friend, a sister—sometimes encouraging, sometimes calling us to account, sometimes challenging, but always present and pointing us beyond ourselves to the God who loves us unconditionally and forever. She proves that holiness is within our grasp.

Opening Prayer

Dear Therese,
with you I believe that holiness
is the only goal really worth striving for.
Help me to want this,
or at least, to want to want it.

Holiness means living for and with God,
and you found a way
that is full of love and confidence,
a way that is open to everyone, even me,
with all my limitations and weaknesses.

Show me how to trust God as you did,
to find in my life signs of divine love and goodness
and celebrate them joyfully.

Show me how to approach God
as a child approaches a loving parent,
knowing that this Father will give me all good things,
and most especially himself.

Therese, be with me during this retreat
as friend, sister and guide
and share with me the secret of holiness,
a holiness that is accomplished
by living the Good News of Jesus
and finding him present in every event of my day.

And I ask this in Jesus' name. Amen.

O Jesus,
you taught us about the door that will be opened
if only we knock.
You said that we would find what we want
if only we look for it,
that we would get what we ask for
if we humbly stretch out our hands.

Confident in your love and mercy
I ask you to draw me ever closer
until it is you yourself who live and act in me.

Set my heart on fire with love
and transform my life into your own.

I know, I seek, I ask the Father for this
in your name. Amen.
(Adapted from words of Therese)

RETREAT SESSION ONE
You Are Loved

Pause for a few minutes and in your mind's eye see Therese sitting beside you. She wears her dark brown woolen habit and a black veil. Her face is young, calm and strong, "like a female Christ" as one person put it on seeing her photograph. On her lap is an open book containing the psalms, the Gospels and some Old Testament passages she has copied out by hand. Therese loves the Scriptures, for from them she has derived her deep knowledge of God's love and mercy.

Sitting there, she looks up at you and smiles. Everyone remarks on Therese's smile; it lights up her whole face. She radiates candor and friendliness, but you can see in her eyes that she has suffered a great deal. Hers has not been an easy path.

Therese wants to share with you the secret of holiness as she discovered it, the way of spiritual childhood. It is based on her grasp of the amazing truth that we are loved by God; from that knowledge flows everything she has to say today: *"You are loved."* Listen as she speaks to you now with simplicity yet with burning conviction. You are loved by God: That is the rock upon which you must build your life. It is the sure basis of holiness.

Therese Speaks

What I want to share with you more than anything else is that you are loved by God. And God has given each one of you "a spirit of power and of love and of self-discipline."[3] Each one of us has a unique story that enfleshes God's care for us. We are valuable and beloved, precious children whom God regards with delight. That's not always easy to believe because our human experience of love is always limited and conditional.

I was fortunate; my early childhood was wonderfully happy. Thus God saw to it that I had a solid foundation that isn't given to everyone. I remember my parents and sisters as always having time for me, hugging me, talking to me, listening to my ideas. Because I was the youngest of the family, I felt especially loved. This love didn't have to be earned or merited, it was there for me just because I was "little Therese," part of the Martin family. I didn't have to try to be good so as to be loved. It was because I knew myself loved that I wanted to respond by being good and giving others joy, not pain. My parents wanted me to be a "little saint."

My sensitive nature had plenty of opportunity to expand during the first four years of my life—before Mama died and the world grew dark. Nearly every day Papa would take me walking with him. On Sundays Mama would join us (at other times she was generally too busy with the lacemaking business to come along). I reveled in the Normandy countryside, the sight of the standing crops dotted with poppies and cornflowers, the trees sweeping the ground with their great branches, the quiet stream where my father fished for hours with me sitting silently beside him, listening to distant music wafted to me over the breeze. I felt so secure it wasn't difficult then to believe in the love of God when I was told of it, child though I was. Everything around me seemed to speak of divine goodness and care.

But life didn't go on in this manner. There was a terribly difficult period after Mama died and we moved to Lisieux. I lost all my self-confidence and retreated into a shell to protect my heart from further pain. I couldn't get on well with other children of my own age. I was bullied at school and found it hard to make friends.

But even during those years I never had cause to doubt my family's love for me. It was, however, a "soft" love, not a challenging one. Maybe God thought I needed time before being made to grow up. Even though I felt awkward and a failure with others, I continued to have confidence in God because my family always supported me. At the time of my First Communion I gave Jesus my heart with great joy and resolution, weak and weepy girl though I was.

I recognize now that grace was always there for me, that God gave me graces freely. I know perfectly well I hadn't earned them, any more than I had earned the gift of my family and the loving support of my father and sisters. These were given without my having to be "worthy." In this way I came to understand while I was still young that God's love is like that too. Everything is gift.

But even as I say this I remember my middle sister, Leonie. She did not feel loved because for some reason she did not know how to please Mama and Papa. She was awkward and difficult and plain to look at. Twice she was expelled from school because her teachers could do nothing with her. Perhaps some of you may identify with her?

My good behavior, then, must have been in some way natural to me. That too was a grace. It's strange how people differ, but I was fortunate. I knew myself loved and realized early (though not yet in a way I could put into words) that God, who accepts us just as we are, loves everyone that way.

This truth came home to me again much later when I was in Carmel and counseling the novices. One of the sisters had had a really terrible childhood. She had been left an orphan and shunted around to different families as a servant. Her experience was almost entirely of abuse and ill treatment. Eventually a priest friend advised her to enter a convent and she came here. She wasn't an easy person to deal with, I can tell you! She had never known security and affection and couldn't believe they were being offered to her, either by God or by us (and these two aspects are intimately related). She would run off and hide when she was supposed to come for a talk with me. She had a tremendous struggle with herself because she always saw the dark side of things. And no wonder! Her very upbringing made it hard for her to relate with the sisters, even though she wanted to.

Did that mean that there was no chance of holiness for her? Not at all! I wanted to help her see that God loved her and was pleased with her attempt to answer the call to holiness. What had happened in her life wasn't as important as how she responded to those happenings, painful and humiliating as they were.

I believed God loved Madeleine (for that was her name) as unconditionally and tenderly as those more gifted. I tried to get this through to her in a thousand different ways, because without the conviction that one is loved, one follows rules from fear. When fear takes hold there is no sense of freedom or joy. Only the knowledge of being loved enables people to respond freely from the heart.

The universal reality is that each one is loved uniquely, tenderly, unrepeatably, as it says in Scripture:

I have loved you with an everlasting love;
therefore I have continued my faithfulness to you.[4]

I so wanted Madeleine to understand that we just have to

allow ourselves to be children once more, to allow ourselves to be carried and loved, abandoning ourselves fearlessly into the arms of our heavenly Father.

"Let whoever is a little one come to me" said the Holy Spirit through the lips of Solomon; and this same Holy Spirit has said *"Mercy is given to little ones."* The prophet Isaiah reveals that on the last day *"the Lord will lead his flock to pasture, he will gather the young lambs and press them to his heart."* And as if all these promises were not enough, the same prophet, whose inspired gaze pierces the eternal depths, cries out in the name of the Lord; *"As a mother caresses her babe, so will I console you. You will be carried at my breast and I will caress you on my knees."* After reading such words there is nothing left but to be silent and shed tears of gratitude and love.

If only all weak and imperfect souls felt as I do, I who am the least of them all, none would despair of arriving at the summit of love's mountain.[5]

All we have to do is to let God love us and carry us as a mother carries and nourishes her child—just because the child is hers and she treasures it unspeakably, even before it can recognize, much less repay, such tenderness.

I knew this deep down and so I could face the suffering that came my way in the struggle for holiness. I wanted to be holy not for my own satisfaction but in response to a loving God. It wasn't always easy to keep this truth before my eyes. As a girl I had a neurotic temperament. Then, when I entered Carmel, there were the years of Papa's mental illness to cope with as well as humiliating difficulties with convent life and relationships. I knew well enough that I wasn't perfect. I could so easily have given in to discouragement and sat down, saying, "What's the use?" But I understood that holiness is about love. And true love embraces whatever suffering is necessary and unavoidable. By embracing pain, we rob it of some of its sting.

One day when I was nearing the end of my life and feeling absolutely bereft and forsaken by God, I was in the garden, walking very slowly because of my weakness and constant pain. Suddenly I saw a hen at the side of the path, hustling her newborn chicks out of my way, protecting them with outstretched wings. I thought of how God had loved and protected me, how God wants indeed to envelop everyone with the tender protectiveness of that mother hen. I was so moved that my eyes filled up with tears and I had to look away. That's how God loves you, too—no matter what it feels like, no matter what kind of personal history you have.

If you want holiness, build your foundation on this rock of God's love. Then your heart will expand and you'll be able to receive this gift that God wants to give you.

A practical way that helped me develop my sense of love and trust in a good God was that I tried to have an attitude of gratitude. There were many good things to thank God for—my parents and sisters, my home, my love of natural beauty, artistic gifts.... But there were other things, too, that I tried to thank God for—things that weren't easy to integrate into the total picture: my mother's early death from cancer; my inability to make friends of my own age; my loss of Pauline, my "second Mama"; my father's long illness; my struggle to break a passionate attachment to my superior that could easily have become an obsession and made a slave of me. I gave thanks for the years when I couldn't feel God near, when I found it hard to believe in God's love—especially when I was dying at twenty-four and felt my whole life had been the pursuit of a mirage, that God didn't even really exist.

Yes, in all these happenings I thanked God and said that I believed everything was the gift of divine love, of

God's plan for me.

To foster this attitude, I trained myself to thank God for a thousand little things every day: for the wildflowers that come in bouquets, for the sun, the silky skin of a peach, the smile of a companion, the snow that fell unexpectedly on the day I received the Carmelite habit.

It is the spirit of gratitude that draws down upon us the overflow of God's grace. No sooner have we thanked him for a blessing than he speedily sends us ten additional gifts. When we thank him for these he multiplies blessings to such a degree that we seem to be under a constant stream of divine graces all coming our way.[6]

If we foster this spirit of gratitude, it is easier to love our way into holiness. This is a constant refrain in Scripture, one that takes us out of ourselves and turns us Godward.

> It is good to give thanks to the LORD,
>   to sing praises to your name, O Most High;
> to declare your steadfast love in the morning,
>   and your faithfulness by night.[7]
>
> O give thanks to the Lord, for he is good
>   for his steadfast love endures for ever.[8]

I've always tried to see the good side of things, even when they were hard and painful. Above all, I've found matter for gratitude in the promises God has made to "little ones"—ordinary people like me whom God calls to friendship, to true holiness. I had some talents: I could write and draw a bit, and I had a sound intelligence. But I was no great intellectual genius or reformer. I had no college degree. I wasn't an angel of charity to the needy or a social worker. My attainments were of the common kind. I had a good share of weaknesses and faults. As a child, I had temper tantrums and I remained obstinate to some degree throughout my life. Yet I never let any of that convince me that holiness was beyond me.

I searched the Scriptures and discovered there that God does not choose "worthy" people, God just calls people like the apostles or Mary Magdalene. Why? They had nothing to boast about on their own account. God even chose Israel purely from love, not because the people had "earned" favor.

So I have wanted to thank God and praise God's mercy to me and others like me: "nobodies" whom God still chooses, loves unconditionally and calls to holiness. Learning to be grateful is one of the first steps to realizing God's love for you.

A Call to Love

Spiritual writer William Johnston says in *Silent Music* that Christian contemplation begins with the realization that we are loved. It does not depend on our initiative, our energy or our vigorous efforts. It depends on our awakening to the reality that God has loved us. "This love, prayerfully experienced, has been compared to the call of the Good Shepherd inviting us to enter his sheepfold," he writes.[9]

In *Crime and Punishment*, Dostoyevsky shows us Rashkolnikov, the murderer, being "reborn" when he is able at last to acknowledge the faithful love of Sonia, who has followed him into Siberia and remained beside him even when there was no spark of response on his part.

How it happened he did not know, but suddenly something seemed to seize him and throw him at her feet. He embraced her knees and wept. At first she was terribly frightened, and her face was covered by a deathly pallor. She jumped to her feet and, trembling all over, looked at him. But at once and at the same moment she understood everything. Her eyes shone with intense happiness; she understood, and she had no doubts at all about it, that he loved her, loved her infinitely, and that the moment she had waited for so long had come at last.

They wanted to speak but could not; tears stood in their eyes. They were both pale and thin; but in those sick and pale faces the dawn of a new future, of a full resurrection to a new life, was already shining. It was love that brought them back to life: the heart of one held inexhaustible sources of life for the other.[10]

After this encounter, Rashkolnikov was able to face a future of suffering and waiting. He was strengthened to pay the price of his regeneration. And what is more, as he looked at the New Testament, he wondered whether Sonia's convictions could also be his. Wonder, joy, humility, gratitude, flooded his being. Sonia's love was the catalyst that gave him a new vision and a new beginning.

That call, that realization, is being offered to us now—by God.

For Reflection

- *Ponder the passage from Therese on page 30 reading it slowly and prayerfully several times. Ask God to help you really believe in the divine love for you and to heal any wounds from the past that hinder your coming to God in a spirit of trust and confidence.*

- *See yourself as a child in God's arms. Let God gaze upon you with tenderness. How do you feel now? How can you respond to this love?*

- *Is there even one incident in your life when you felt really loved? How did you react? It is said that "perfect love casts out fear"; do you think this is true from your own experience? Have you felt it necessary to "earn" love from God, parents, friends? If so, did it generate anxiety? Lack of peace? Fearfulness?*

- *Write a personal litany of gratitude, thanking God for being with you in all events of your life and for giving you so many blessings.*

Closing Prayer

O my God, I believe in your love for me—
a love more tender than a mother's love,
more strong and true than any earthly father could
     give.
Help me to base my life on the knowledge
that your love is always there for me,
given freely and without condition.

Secure in your love
may I not be afraid to look
at all areas of my past life
and find there matter for gratitude.
Whatever my past, you were there with me.
Whatever is present now is your gift.
Whatever happens in the future
is safe in your hands.

Help me to realize that you have given me
all I need to be holy

in my daily life,
and that you want holiness for me
more than I can want it myself.

My God, I trust you,
I love you,
I have confidence in you
and in your love for me.
Make this the one reality of my life,
as it was the guiding star of Therese's life.
And I ask this in the name of Jesus, our Lord. Amen.

Jesus,
My gratitude bids me say
that you love me fondly.
When I meet with such love from you
how can my heart fail to go out to you?
How can my trust in you have any limits?—Therese

Notes

[1] "Letter CXXI," July 6, 1893.

[2] *A Memoir of My Sister*, by Sr. Genevieve of the Holy Face (Celine), p. 23.

[3] 2 Timothy 1:7b.

[4] Jeremiah 31:3.

[5] "Letter to Marie."

[6] *Memoir*, p. 97.

[7] Psalm 92:1.

[8] Psalm 107:1.

[9] William Johnston, *Silent Music* (Collins, 1974), p. 117.

[10] Fyodor Dostoyevsky, *Crime and Punishment*, trans. D. Magarshack (Penguin, 1951), pp. 557-558.

Day Two
Have Confidence in Love

Coming Together in the Spirit

Therese is sitting with us once more. This time Madeleine herself is in the group. The sunlight streams in through the open window, lighting up Madeleine's face, but she doesn't raise her eyes or enjoy the warmth of it. She looks withdrawn and sulky.

Yes, Madeleine says, she has heard all Therese has been saying about God's love, but she hasn't found much in her own life for which to be thankful. She understands everything in her head, but somehow she doesn't feel anything in her heart.

Maybe at some point in the future she will have come to terms with some of the past wounds, Madeleine says; meanwhile she needs to get herself together, experience some better, more fulfilling relationships, read and study more Scripture. Then she will feel more able to face the Lord, then she will feel more lovable.

Therese listens carefully to the troubled novice. She doesn't make light of Madeleine's problem (or ours, if we share it). Instead she gently draws Madeleine's head down onto her breast in a loving gesture and tells the following story.

A King who had set out on the chase noticed his dogs

pursuing a small white rabbit which was just ahead of them.

When the little rabbit began to sense that the dogs were about to pounce on it, it turned suddenly and bounded back, jumping into the arms of the huntsman.

Deeply moved by this show of confidence the king from then on cherished the rabbit as his own. He allowed no one to molest it and nourished and cared for the little animal himself.[1]

"You see, no matter how helpless we feel, we have only to leap up into God's arms. Then he will be so touched, as it were, by our confidence that he cannot help but repay our act of trust."

Defining Our Thematic Context

In Day One we looked at the truth that God has loved us first, and that God's love is total, unconditional and unique to each person. Today we'll explore how we can make this more of a reality in our lives right now.

We can feel weighted down by difficulties, with problems we can't shake off, pursued by a past that is always catching up with us. In the future maybe we will turn to God, but right now we aren't ready.

But the whole point of Therese's story is that the little rabbit is doing the only possible thing if it wants to survive. Like that little animal, we must throw ourselves into God's arms with confidence and give God the opportunity to prove absolute reliability and trustworthiness. But we tend to hang back, thinking either that God is not merciful enough or that we haven't yet made the grade.

It is confidence and confidence alone that leads to

love, says Therese. We cannot know another's trustworthiness unless we actually do trust, making the leap of faith. Only then do we discover the truth for ourselves. God is merciful and loving, and will not disappoint our hopes. We can have absolute confidence in God.

Opening Prayer

> My God,
> I want to have confidence in your love
> but so many things seem to hold me back:
> past wounds, past hurts, past betrayals,
> past sins—mine and others'.
>
> Open my eyes.
> Open my heart.
> Enable me to take the leap of faith
> that is needed now.
>
> Holiness isn't a matter of starting to love you
> sometime in the future,
> or even tomorrow.
> I don't have to wait until I become a better person,
> holier, more worthy, more virtuous.
> It's a matter of trusting in your mercy *today*,
>   just as I am.
>
> You showed this to Therese;
> show me, too,
> and give me a spirit of great confidence.
>
> I ask this through Jesus,
> your beloved Son and our merciful Savior.
> Amen.

RETREAT SESSION TWO
Confidence

In this session Therese will explore the theme of confidence under three aspects:

Accepting yourself as you are *now*.
Coming to God as you are *now*.
Praying as you are *now*.

She is here with us, waiting quietly for our attention before she begins to speak.

Therese Speaks

You've heard my story of the little rabbit, but I didn't always understand that God is more pleased with our trust than anything else. Like most people, I thought I had to become a saintly sort of person before I could claim God's love and mercy.

I used to think that being holy meant being "perfect"— never feeling angry or rebellious, always being obedient, avoiding simple pleasures. Can you believe that as a girl I even felt guilty because I had new blue ribbons in my hair and looked nice!

I couldn't live fully because I was afraid of all sorts of things. I hadn't yet discovered the power of love, which takes you out of yourself and launches you into a deep sea, way out of your depths. Instead I was paddling along in the shallows, wrapped up in trying to be virtuous. Indeed, I felt quite superior to my sister Leonie, who rebelled against all this good behavior and showed her frustration in various ways. She refused to live by all the "convent rules" our parents set before us.

You see, I had a lot of growing up to do. I needed to become free, released from self-centered scrupulosity. For this I had to discover the Jesus of the Gospels as well as the real Therese beneath the veneer. In today's terms I needed to accept and befriend my shadow side—my unacceptable feelings, my inability to cope. I had to understand how much I needed God before God's grace could triumph.

Fortunately, God gives each one of us opportunities to grow up and face reality. I was given many in Carmel. That's when I began to realize the meaning of true holiness and not the counterfeit kind that puts people off.

Trusting at each step, I let God show me how far I was from my goal. My eyes were opened to my weaknesses and God gave me the courage to look hard at them.

For example, some of the sisters really got on my nerves with their annoying mannerisms and snide remarks. I discovered that I wasn't as patient and loving as I had thought! I was sensitive and easily hurt. Then I found myself becoming emotionally attached to the prioress in an unhealthy way and had to struggle with all sorts of new feelings. I wasn't good at my tasks and left cobwebs around when cleaning. (I didn't see them but others did!)

And what can I say of my father's illness and the agony that brought me? My heart was bleeding with sorrow and there wasn't much sympathy given to the daughter of a man confined in a mental asylum.

In other words, I had to accept that I was only a weak human being, and I couldn't surmount my difficulties just by willing to do so. I couldn't say, "From now on I won't let the sisters hurt me. I'll conquer my emotional problems and not worry about what people say about

Papa," and so on. I just felt as if I were down on the ground, crushed, a nobody, a grain of sand—not the little queen I had been.

And that's how I had to come to Jesus, not all beautiful and virtuous, not a ready-made saint, but a sinner—a creature liable to make mistakes, a rather repressed young woman who found many aspects of life hard and bitter.

I realized that I truly needed God's mercy. I had to stretch out my hands for help, confident it would be given. What's more important, I had to do it *now*, and not wait until I felt better, stronger, more virtuous.

I learned to pray from my heart in words like these: *We want never to fall?— What does it matter, my Jesus, if I fall at every instant, for thereby I see my weakness and that, for me, is great gain. Thereby you see what I can do, and so you will be moved to carry me in your arms.... If you do not, it is because it pleases you to see me on the ground...so I shall not be disquieted but shall go on stretching out to you the arms of supplications and love! I cannot believe that you would abandon me!*[2]

Holiness is compatible with weakness and imperfection. Being weak is its own grace. *When in the morning we feel no courage or strength for the practice of virtue—then is the moment to put the ax to the root of the tree.*[3]

So come to God now, as you are. Don't be surprised that you are frail and wounded. For today grace will be given. Turn your failures, your difficulties, your sufferings into acts of love and confidence instead of sinking into despair and anxiety.

I can assure you, holiness is within our grasp—within your grasp, just as you are. Only accept yourself and the opportunities to be a loving person that today offers.

[Therese pauses and opens the book of the Gospels she always keeps beside her. She turns to Luke 15:11-32 and reads the parable of the Prodigal Son. Hear her reading this familiar story of forgiveness and reconciliation. Quietly ponder it from the point of view of the younger son, the elder son, the father.]

Then Jesus said, "There was a man who had two sons. The younger of them said to his father, "Father, give me the share of the property that will belong to me." So he divided his property between them. A few days later the younger son gathered all he had and traveled to a distant country, and there he squandered his property in dissolute living. When he had spent everything, a severe famine took place throughout that country, and he began to be in need. So he went and hired himself out to one of the citizens of that country, who sent him to his fields to feed the pigs. He would gladly have filled himself with the pods that the pigs were eating; and no one gave him anything. But when he came to himself he said, 'How many of my father's hired hands have bread enough and to spare, but here I am dying of hunger! I will get up and go to my father, and I will say to him, "Father, I have sinned against heaven and before you; I am no longer worthy to be called your son; treat me like one of your hired hands."' So he set off and went to his father. But while he was still far off, his father saw him and was filled with compassion; he ran and put his arms around him and kissed him. Then the son said to him, 'Father, I have sinned against heaven and before you; I am no longer worthy to be called your son.' But the father said to his slaves, 'Quickly, bring out a robe—the best one—and put it on him; put a ring on his finger and sandals on his feet. And get the fatted calf and kill it, and let us eat and celebrate; for this son of mine was dead and is alive again; he was lost and is found!' And they began to celebrate.

"Now his elder son was in the field; and when he came and approached the house, he heard music and dancing. He called one of the slaves and asked what was going on. 'Your brother has come, and your father has killed the fatted calf, because he has got him back safe and sound.' Then he became angry and refused to go in. His father came out and began to plead with him. But he answered his father, 'Listen! For all these years I have been working like a slave for you, and I have never disobeyed your command; yet you have never given me even a young goat so that I might celebrate with my friends. But when this son of yours came back, who has devoured your property with prostitutes, you killed the fatted calf for him!' Then the father said to him, 'Son, you are always with me, and all that is mine is yours. But we had to celebrate and rejoice, because this brother of yours was dead and has come to life; he was lost and has been found.' "

This parable assures us that God is tender and compassionate, and that's the God I believe in.

The younger son has behaved abominably. He has hurt his father and wasted his share of the family money in loose living. It's only when he finds himself completely destitute that he decides to go home, and then only because he wants something to eat. He gets up and goes back, just as he is, starving and ragged, ready to do any menial tasks his father might set him.

But the father has been waiting, watching, longing for his son's return. He sees him in the distance and runs out, clasping the ashamed and wretched young man to his heart, organizing a big party, ordering the best clothes, wanting everyone to rejoice "because my son was dead and has come back to life, he was lost and is found!"

It's the elder son who isn't pleased because to him this

doesn't seem fair at all! He has been good, worked hard, done everything he ought to do. Why doesn't he get a party?

This son has missed the point. He is always with the father. Everything the father has belongs to him. But he is self-righteous, unable to be pleased at another's homecoming. He can't understand why forgiveness, not punishment, awaits the rebel.

When I look at those two sons I see two aspects of myself. One is the good elder son, who does what he should and remains with the father always; the other is the wastrel. The father loves them both, but his deepest compassion is for the younger one who realizes his need for mercy and forgiveness. And *I'm certain of this—that if my conscience were burdened with all the sins it's possible to commit, I would still go and throw myself into our Lord's arms, my heart all broken up with sorrow. I know what tenderness he has for any prodigal child that comes back to him.*[4]

We need to believe in forgiveness. We don't find it enough in human relationships, even between parent and child, husband and wife, brother and sister, friend and friend. So we project mean ideas of conditional forgiveness onto God instead of looking long and hard at stories like that of the Prodigal Son and noting how Jesus himself welcomed sinners.

Think of what may be on your own conscience right now. Are you weighed down by fear, by burdens, by a broken relationship? By the guilt of sin, real or imaginary? Have you neglected an elderly parent? Had an abortion? Failed to reach out to those in need? Abused your own or others' bodies? Or has your sin been like that of the elder son—being self-satisfied, hard-hearted, judgmental? Maybe your burden consists of an accumulation of so-called "little things": harboring thoughts of revenge or dislike, gossiping, being addicted to food or drink, giving way to racial or religious prejudice.

Whatever weighs you down from the past, the gospel message is the same: Come back to God, come now. Accept the forgiveness and grace that is offered for free. And what's more, you give joy to God just by accepting this invitation. You don't have to promise never to sin again. Jesus doesn't lay down conditions, but accepts you as you are—now. And he will continue to accept you, no matter how many times you fall and get up. *Why should it frighten you that you cannot bear his cross without weakening? On the way to Calvary Jesus fell three times; and you, would you not fall a hundred times, if need be, to prove your love by rising up again with more strength than before your fall?*[5]

It offends our human judgment, doesn't it, that no penalty is exacted from the prodigal; that the father forgives totally and rehabilitates completely. There is no anger, reproof, blame or punishment. Everything is forgiven. Period. It sounds too good to be true, but is true. *I cannot understand those who are afraid of so loving a friend. For those who love him and, after each discourteous act cast themselves into his arms, Jesus is vibrant with joy.*[6]

Let's look at a similar story through gospel eyes:

A bus was traveling south. A woman passenger noticed that the man beside her was becoming increasingly restless and nervous, looking out of the window and away again, unable to concentrate on the magazine he held and only pretending to read. At last she asked him if something was bothering him, and he told her his story.

"I've just come out of prison in New York state, paroled after a murder. My wife's in South Carolina and I haven't heard from her in ages—we're not much good at writing, you see. I'm hoping she'll have me back, so I got a mate to send a postcard saying I'd be on this bus sometime this week. If she's willing to have me back, maybe she'd tie a yellow rag onto the tree in our yard. If I see it when the bus passes by, I'll get off. If not, I'll just ride straight on and make a new life for myself somewhere else. We're getting close now. I'm afraid I'm too nervous to look. You look and tell me if you see anything; it's just around the corner."

The woman glanced apprehensively out of the window as the bus turned the corner, then her gaze widened and she hugged the man, pointing excitedly. There was the tree, with a mass of yellow silk ribbons waving gaily from every branch like a gigantic bunch of flowers.

Tears filled the man's eyes. "Oh, she wants me, she loves me!" he murmured. He got off the bus and ran joyfully and confidently into his wife's arms.

Did that man hesitate when he saw the ribbons? Did he doubt his wife's love? No. And neither should we. The yellow ribbons are on God's tree whenever we want to come home, whatever we may have done.

But for that we have to be humble. For myself, I absolutely refused to be paralyzed by guilt feelings. I saw that distorted emotions, feelings of worthlessness and uselessness were just that—feelings, not the truth of the matter.

How could I be bogged down in resentment and self-pity or be concerned about my self-image when I'm invited, just as I am, to a joyful homecoming? God is far kinder than you think. Don't wait to become holy. Grasp the holiness offered by coming home, and coming now.

There is just one more question on this day devoted to

confidence. What about prayer? I dedicated myself to a life of prayer. Do you think that means I have had exceptional graces? What did I do at prayer? How did I express my love and confidence in God?

Without prayer there can be no genuine holiness, but often we feel at sea when we go to pray. Nearly all my time in Carmel I've had a real struggle with formal prayer.

As a girl I thought prayer meant feeling good about being with God, finding it easy to be silent and just love God. But as soon as I became a nun all those feelings of love seemed to evaporate and I had to discover what loving God really means. It's about choosing God, giving God time—not just when I want, but regularly.

I was never one of those people who could sit still and "contemplate." I've never experienced a vision or an ecstasy. I walked the path of prayer most people walk, the ordinary path.

One thing I'm convinced of is that giving God time is important for holiness. It's one way of showing that I need God, and can do nothing without God. Jesus said this himself. That meant I gave time to God, to prayer, even when I felt discouraged or tired or seemed to get no feedback. You see, *many serve Jesus when he consoles them, but few are willing to keep him company sleeping on the waves of suffering or in the garden of the agony. Who is really willing to serve Jesus for himself? It must be you and I.*[7]

So I allowed Jesus to sleep if he wanted. (And indeed I often slept in his presence myself!)

Each day I read and pondered the Gospels, and during my work I tried to speak with Jesus as a friend and companion. I did this naturally and simply, sharing my worries and concerns, my joys and sorrows. I wanted to make him part of my life at every moment.

It's a mistake to imagine that your prayer won't be

answered unless you have something out of a book, some
splendid formula of words specially devised to meet an
emergency. I can't face the strain of hunting about in books for
splendid prayers—it makes my head spin.

I do what children have to do before they have learned to
read. I tell God quite simply what I want without any splendid
turns of phrase.

For me, prayer means lifting up one's eyes quite simply to
heaven, a cry of grateful love, from the crest of joy or the trough
of despair.[8]

I never manage to say the rosary well. I find it more
helpful to say just one Our Father or Hail Mary really
slowly to set me back on course.

At other times I liken myself to a little bird hopping
around under the Sun of Love—often distracted by
trifles, often asleep, often weak and imperfect. No great
eagle by any reckoning! But I stay at my post, looking not
at myself, but upward at the sun, believing it to be there
even when it is hidden behind the clouds. That's real
trust!

When I was in an agony as my tuberculosis worsened,
a sister asked me, "What do you say to God?" I told her,
"I say nothing—I just love him."

So don't wait until you feel ready to pray, full of
fervor, full of good thoughts and holy desires. Instead,
pray in any way you can, right now.

A Call to Love

The kernel of Therese's teaching on confidence is that,
by meditating on the God Jesus reveals in the Gospels, we
are enabled to trust. God is merciful, God is love, so we
can run to God, vulnerable and undefended, knowing
that we will always be received with forgiveness and

kindness. As Marcus Borg writes in *Jesus: A New Vision*:

> If we see reality as hostile, indifferent, or "judge,"
> then self-preservation becomes the first law of our
> being. We must protect ourselves against reality and
> make ourselves secure in the face of its threats,
> whether we choose secular or religious means to do
> so. But if we see reality as supportive and
> nourishing, then another response to life becomes
> possible: trust. To say that God is gracious means
> that the relationship with God is not dependent
> upon performance as measured by the standards of
> conventional wisdom. The relationship is prior to
> that. In traditional religious language God loves and
> is gracious to people prior to any achievement on
> their part; in more religiously neutral language,
> reality is marked by a cosmic generosity. But we do
> not commonly see it that way. We typically live our
> lives as if reality were not gracious.[9]

Therese saw—God wants us to see—reality as gracious,
as impregnated through and through with love. She
refused to be afraid and felt no need to hold any part of
herself back just for herself.

Step by step she built up her spirit of confidence in
God, knowing that at each moment she would receive all
that she needed for spiritual growth, wholeness and
holiness.

For Reflection

- *Do you know your own strengths and weaknesses? Are
  your ideas of perfection unreal, out of touch with the kind of
  person God has made you? Ask Jesus to show you more
  clearly how you can be holy in the way he wants you to be.*

- *When you pray, what practical aids help you to remain in God's presence: reading Scripture, vocal prayer, silent contemplation? With Therese, try saying the Our Father slowly and prayerfully. Set yourself some regular time for daily prayer and keep to it no matter how you feel.*

- *What holds you back from accepting the love and forgiveness God offers to you now? Whatever it may be, try to throw it behind you and run into God's arms.*

- *Has your religious upbringing been narrow, cramping, full of fear? If so, what steps can you take to remedy this? Ask Therese to be with you as you open yourself to further growth in understanding.*

Closing Prayer

My God,
Jesus revealed you as a waiting Father,
full of compassion and love,
ever ready to welcome
anyone who turns to you.

I believe that you accept me just as I am;
help me to accept myself.
I believe that your arms are open to receive me,
help me to cast myself into them.
I believe that you hear me
even before I begin to pray
and that you know my heart's deepest desires.

You are with me here right now,
loving me, forgiving me,
finding joy in my being with you.
And so I can come to you with great confidence
knowing that all you want is my trust

and my love—*today*. Amen.

My life is an instant, a passing hour,
My life is a moment escaping away,
You know, my God, that to love you upon earth
I have only today.

What matters it, Lord, if dark the future hover?
One prayer for tomorrow—O no, I cannot say.
My heart untouched preserve and with your shadow cover
If only for today.—Therese

Notes

[1] *Memoir*, p. 59.
[2] "Letter LXV," April 26, 1888.
[3] "Letter XL."
[4] *Autobiography*, Chapter XL.
[5] "Letter LVII," January 1889.
[6] "Letter CCXXXI," July 26, 1894.
[7] "Letter CXLIV," July 7, 1894.
[8] *Autobiography*, Chapter XXXVII.
[9] *Jesus: A New Vision*, by Marcus Borg (SPCK, 1993), p. 103.

DAY THREE
Courage to Conquer

Coming Together in the Spirit

Today Therese pokes her head around the door and gives us a start! She doesn't look like her usual self. There's a mop of fair hair hanging around her impish face, and as she steps through the opening we can see that, though she is wearing her brown habit, she has on over it stiff silver paper cut to look like armor—and she's carrying a cardboard sword. At closer quarters we can see that the long hair is a wig fixed atop her white linen head covering. So what's the fancy costume for?

"Just thought I'd give you a jolt." She laughs. "It's me acting Joan of Arc in a play I wrote to entertain the sisters. From the way I'm depicted in art, delicately holding flowers, I'm sure you didn't expect me to have chosen Joan of Arc as my special patron. But I have done so."

Therese continues: "The little way I'm talking about, the way of confidence and love, doesn't just drop into anyone's lap, and it didn't drop into mine. I had to fight hard, I'll tell you.

"If we want holiness we must never give up, but fight on with whatever weapons come to hand, confident that all the help we need will be given moment by moment. It's making the effort that counts. Making the effort shows we want the Lord more than we want our own selfish satisfaction.

"Remember the musical *My Fair Lady*, in which Eliza Doolittle tries and tries to speak correctly. Then suddenly one day the right words, the right pronunciation seem to flow effortlessly off her tongue: 'The rain in Spain falls mainly in the plain.' And Eliza and everyone else rejoice. It looks effortless now, but before that has gone hours of practice and seeming failure.

"Maybe it's a bit like riding a bicycle. You get up on the seat, wobble and fall off, wobble and fall off. But if you persevere, suddenly the balance seems perfect—and off you go, free as a bird."

Defining Our Thematic Context

This session focuses on wanting holiness enough to conquer all obstacles in our way.

Therese assures us that if we want holiness we can have it. But we must show our earnestness, our real desire for this gift, by being ready to fight, confident that in God's good time we will gain the victory.

The victory means happiness and freedom—even if, like Joan of Arc, we have to suffer the flames in one way or another.

Opening Prayer

My God,
today is a new day,
a day to draw closer to you,
a day in which to love you more,
a day to gain the victory over self
out of love for you.

With Therese as my teacher
show me how to go forward with courage,
ready to conquer all obstacles
despite my many weaknesses.

"For you are a God of the lowly,
helper of the oppressed
upholder of the weak,
protector of the forsaken,
savior of those without hope."[1]

And I ask this in Jesus' name. Amen

RETREAT SESSION THREE

Aim High

Because of Therese, thousands of other ordinary
people (people who, like you and me, think they are too
ordinary to be "holy") have been given an assurance that
no matter what spiritual, physical or emotional
handicaps they bear, they can be all God wants them to
be. Therese turned everything—depression, neurosis,
loneliness, terminal illness—into a loving prayer of
acceptance. This is the kind of courage she hopes we will
emulate.

Remember the maxim of Saint John of the Cross:
"Think on this only, that all is ordained by God. And do
you love where there's no love and you'll draw love out."

Therese Speaks

Trying to be honest with myself, I knew that wishing and willing are two different things. Everyone would like to be more loving. Most of us wish we could pray more regularly, conquer our pride, be free of character faults, overcome our addictions and compulsions. But do we will it? Are we prepared to take practical steps to do what we can? Do we will the means and not just the end?

Let me tell you about an incident that was a turning point in my own life.

I was a weepy and self-centered girl; *really my touchiness in those days was quite unbearable* [2] and, being the youngest, I never did my share of the housework. I began to try helping others, but if my efforts were not appreciated I burst into tears.

If I had given some slight annoyance to anyone I was fond of without in the least meaning to, it was obvious that crying about it only made things worse, but could I control myself? No, I wept like the Magdalene herself, and as soon as I'd begun to cheer up about what I'd done, I started crying about having cried over it. Arguments were unavailing; nothing would cure me of this unpleasant habit. [3] What a child I was!

I expect you can think of some aspect of your own character that is somewhat similar, something you just don't seem able to master. Maybe it is a tendency to bad temper, impatience, over-submissiveness or jealousy.

Anyway, the Christmas I was nearly fourteen my shoes were still being placed in the chimney corner for me to find them filled with sweets and little gifts after Midnight Mass. I was running upstairs happily to take off my pretty white hat and matching muff when I heard my father exclaim in an irritable voice to Celine, "Therese should have grown out of this ritual by now. Thank goodness this will be the last year."

Well, I felt dreadful. Papa hadn't meant me to hear but I had, and Celine, who was following me upstairs realized it. Knowing what a weeper I was, she urged me not to go down for a while. I would only upset Papa with my tears.

But suddenly I found myself with new strength. I ran down and opened my gifts with cries of delight. Papa, his good humor restored, looked on indulgently. *In a single instant our Lord brought about the change that I had vainly tried to achieve these ten years past. I'd tried and that was enough for him.*

Quite simply, charity had found its way into my heart, calling on me to forget myself and simply do what was wanted of me; and since then I've been happy as the day is long.[4]

Those ten years of trying and failing bore fruit. And having gained one victory, I was ready for further battles that would lead me toward freedom. I look back to that Christmas as a time of special meaning that gave direction to my future.

Our Lord, newly born, turned this darkness of mine into a flood of light; born to share my human weakness, he brought me the strength and courage I needed. He armed me so well that holy night that I never looked back; I was like a soldier, winning one vantage point after another, like a "great runner who sees the track before him." My tears dried up at their source; they flowed now only at long intervals and with difficulty. Somebody had once said to me: "If you cry like that when you're small, you'll have no tears left later on" and it was true.[5]

Holiness, I realized, had to be won at the point of the sword.

So when I came to Carmel I didn't see it as a peaceful retreat but as a battleground where I would wrestle to gain more ground for God's life to flourish within me and where, as God's life took over, I would be able to draw others to Jesus by the power of prayer and the force of example. I didn't trust in my own strength; instead I put all my trust in Jesus.

I wanted to be another Joan of Arc even though I wasn't fighting battles people could see. I wrote poems and plays in Joan's honor putting my own aspirations into her mouth.

> *The sacrifice I love, the cross in my desire.*
> *O deign to summon me—to suffer here I am.*[6]

I wasn't put off because Joan's life seemed different from mine. Courage can be recognized in any way of life. It's an inner reality and I wanted it.

> *We sing no pride of Joan's victorious hour,*
> *We do not praise the pomp and panoply thereof,*
> *We sing a truer worth, a higher power*
> *Her stainless heart, her martyrdom of love.*[7]

Readiness to fight and conquer was a spiritual goal for me, not a dream without substance. My weapons were love and sacrifice, and I wielded them with sustained effort and practical strategy. My sword was the word of God and I found many people in the Bible to encourage me.

If you look at the stories of Esther and Judith, for example, you'll see two more heroines. Neither woman was especially powerful or gifted, but with God's help they were each ready to do what was demanded by circumstance.

To save her people from a purge, Esther approached her husband, the king, at the peril of her own life even though she was almost paralyzed by fear.

She prayed to the Lord of Israel and said:

O my Lord, you only are our King; help me who am alone and have no helper but you.... Remember, O Lord; make yourself known in this time of our affliction, and give me courage.... O God, whose might is over all, hear the voice of the despairing, and save us from the hands of evildoers. And save me from my fear![8]

Have you ever felt like that and yet done what you knew to be right?

And then, to aid the Israelites, another woman, Judith, a widow, was willing to go unarmed into the enemy camp so as to kill the tyrant Holofernes. She, too, puts her trust in God despite the natural fear she feels as she prays.

Give to me, a widow, the strong hand to do what I plan.... For your strength does not depend on numbers, nor your might on the powerful. But you are the God of the lowly, helper of the oppressed, upholder of the weak, protector of the forsaken, savior of those without hope.[9]

Where do you find yourself in these stories? I can identify with these women, who, like Joan, would have preferred an easier path, yet rose to greatness through their courage, even though they felt afraid.

I'd like to share with you three of my personal struggles that ended in victory. Maybe you'll see yourself in one or more of them. First, I am sure everyone knows people who rub us the wrong way. It's nobody's fault that there seems to be some natural incompatibility between us. It's a fact we must face.

Well, *there's a sister here who has the knack of rubbing me the wrong way at every turn; her tricks of manner, her tricks of speech, her character, just strike me as unlovable.*[10] And I have to live with her day in and day out.

In such an instance, isn't it natural to keep out of the other's way as much as possible, and make friends only among those with whom we feel on the same wavelength?

But pondering over the words of Jesus in the Gospels, "Love one another as I have loved you,"[11] I realized I was a long way from doing what Jesus wanted. Loving people as he loves them is a big enough challenge to last a lifetime!

Love isn't about feelings. It's practical. *Love means putting up with other people's shortcomings, feeling no surprise at their weakness, finding encouragement even in the slightest evidence of good qualities in them.*[12]

But what came home to me most of all was the conviction that love of others doesn't have to be kept hidden in one's heart or given only to a select few. It's like a lamp set on a lampstand. *The cheerful light it radiates isn't meant simply for the people we are fond of; it's meant for everyone in the house without exception.*[13]

So, taking Jesus' words seriously, I decided to treat the sister who annoyed me as though she were my best friend. I prayed for her; at every opportunity I did her a good turn; I often chose to sit beside her and confide in her; I lent a hand whenever she needed help; I smiled at her whenever we met.

In fact, I did so well that this sister truly believed that I loved her the best of all in the community. Even my own sister Marie felt jealous, and complained that I seemed to prefer this person above my blood relations.

You see I had "poured in love" as best I could and so was able to draw love out of a person who otherwise had no friends and who therefore couldn't blossom in the group.

Does this ring any bells with your experience?

Think of how you might do something similar with a neighbor or relative you would rather avoid. Jesus dwells in that person as much as he dwells in you. He or she is loved with a divine love. But most of us need others to reveal that humanly we are lovable and capable of responding. If you reach out to others in love, especially those you don't really care for, you will be doing the work of Jesus himself.

But plan your strategy. Don't just say "I will be kinder." Like me, do something definite. Urge yourself on by remembering the word of Scripture: "Little children, let us love, not in word or speech, but in truth and action."[14]

A second victory I'll tell you about is one that many people face today: over-dependence on others. When we do not dedicate ourselves to becoming spiritually mature, we often allow others to define our identity for us.

I came to Carmel at the age of fifteen, young and with a very affectionate heart. The convent was my new home, but it was strange and lonely at first when I was getting adjusted. My superior was a strong, dominant woman. I felt drawn toward Mother Marie de Gonzague and wanted to give and receive special love and attention from her. Lots of the nuns did. Mother Marie was an aristocrat, attractive and well educated. She showed favoritism to certain sisters, and this was very painful to me. Gradually, I came to see that those who curried favor with Mother Marie were like pet dogs slavishly attached to their owner.

I'd had a little dog of my own, Tom, so I know what I'm talking about. Tom followed me around everywhere, was miserable if I wasn't around, would do special tricks to please me. That's fine for a dog, but people are meant to be free.

My word—what a struggle it was! Every time I passed
Mother Gonzague's room, I wanted to go in and see her.
I thought of a thousand ways I could get her to notice me
and pet me. I had to run past her door and cling to the
banisters, forcing myself not to turn back. I didn't deny
my feelings, but I recognized them for what they were:
immature passions unworthy of an adult.

How grateful I am now that I held firm in those early
days. *The food of real love is sacrifice; just in proportion as you
deny yourself any kind of selfish indulgence, your affection for
the other person becomes something stronger and less
self-regarding.*

*There's a reward promised to people who fight bravely and
I'm glad to say I've got it already. I don't find it necessary any
longer to turn away from any consolation my heart craves,
because I made up my mind to love our Lord above everything
else, and my soul is now fixed in that resolve. I find, to my
great delight, that when you love him the capacities of your
heart are enlarged, so that your feelings toward those who are
dear to you are infinitely more tender than they would have
been if you had devoted yourself to a selfish kind of love which
remains barren.*[15]

I know now from experience that loving God, giving
God first place, brings freedom and joy. Making idols of
other people, no matter how good they are, leads to
misery and slavery.

Think now of your own life. Are you so dependent on
another person that you get jealous if they make other
friends? Are you unhappy if they don't notice you and
praise you? If so, then realize that Jesus is one who will
never disappoint you. Don't build your life on people
whose affections change from day to day. Be free to love
and be loved—you'll find your heart expanding to
embrace the whole world.

And lastly I'll relate to you how I grappled with

a petty annoyance.

It was at my daily prayer time that I found myself kneeling in front of a sister who had a most annoying habit. She would rub her fingernails up and down against her front tooth. This tiny noise drove me crazy.

I felt I needed silence to concentrate on God. *I longed to turn round and give the offender one look; obviously she was quite unconscious of fidgeting and it didn't seem as if there were any other way of letting her know about it. But something told me—something deep down inside me—that the right thing to do was to put up with it for the love of God and spare the sister any embarrassment.*[16]

So I tried to ignore that noise. Impossible! What could I do?

Then I had another idea. I could listen hard and offer the sweet music of tooth and nail to God, making that my prayer. Only then did peace come.

Yes, I know it was a small thing. But our weakness is that we usually want other people to change, or circumstances to change.

As many people of your own time who are involved in Twelve-Step and other recovery programs have realized, we cannot force others to change to suit ourselves. One wise person put it this way: "Our greatest impact on the lives of others is in how we live our lives and not in how we tell them to live theirs."

A Call to Love

Therese's spirituality is characterized by a constant vigilance and energy in responding generously to opportunities to love. Anyone can do what suits his or her own temperament and personality without too much effort. But what of those other aspects of ourselves that we overlook and where we give in to all kinds of selfishness? These areas too must be faced truthfully and courageously.

In his best-selling book, *The Seven Habits of Highly Effective People*, Stephen R. Covey provides "powerful lessons in personal change." He advises readers to ask themselves: What really matters to me? What am I doing and why? Covey recommends simple visualization exercises that can help us answer those questions. For example: College students were asked to assume that they had only one semester left to live and that they were to remain in school as good students. They were then asked to visualize how they would spend that final semester.

The students began writing letters of appreciation for their parents. They sought forgiveness from relatives and friends they had offended. They stopped putting each other down, and tried to be less judgmental. "The dominant, central theme of their activities, the underlying principle," Covey says, "is love."[17]

Once the students had visualized themselves as having only a short time to live, they were able to sort out what really mattered. And they were willing to expend the effort required in loving others, an effort they were willing to renew day by precious day.

Therese was convinced that it is the effort we make to love others that matters. If we fail often, rather than being discouraged we should use this as an opportunity for excusing faults in our neighbor, knowing how often we do not live up to our own unreal expectations. Therese knew how to capitalize on her weaknesses as well as her strengths. She fought on regardless. She felt inadequate and imperfect to the end of her days. But she knew that what mattered was constant trying; victory would come in God's time. The God Therese loved would take care of the outcome.

Therese, wielding the sword of the Spirit, believed absolutely in Jesus' words:

> Ask, and it will be given you; search, and you will
> find; knock, and the door will be opened for you.
> For everyone who asks receives, and everyone who
> searches finds, and for everyone who knocks, the
> door will be opened.[18]

Therese asked, searched and knocked relentlessly—and the door was opened. As she wrote after becoming Mistress of Novices, "*One thing I've noticed is this, all souls, more or less, have to put up the same sort of fight, but on the other hand, no two souls are alike.*"[19]

Therese would agree with the following words:

> There are in this world only potential saints who
> come into actual existence by their own effort,
> through a series of frustrations, trials and failures. It
> is courage that makes the saint; and courage is no
> more than confidence in grace that comes from on
> high and is always available, though we do not
> always open our hearts to receive it.[19]

This sounds as if the saint is strong-willed, but it is not so. Strong will is linked to self-love and a desire for the self to triumph. In holiness the will yields first place to love by putting no obstacle in love's way. So, in some sense, holiness really is natural, a perfecting of our nature. The saint is always in tune with his or her deepest needs and aspirations. It is we who block the way to the true joy of becoming our real selves, remaining slaves instead to our lower impulses. Acceptance of life, abandonment in all circumstances, is the key to sustained growth.

At the end of her life, when people all around were

congratulating Therese on her courage, she only said she had striven to acquire it, looking not at herself but always at God. Jesus' courage had been tested in Gethsemane, and he had gone forward to the cross despite his natural abhorrence. Therese, like him, had tried to say always, "Not my will but yours be done."[20]

Ordinariness can be mistaken for mediocrity. Therese seems "ordinary," but she is not mediocre. She is a sign of hope, challenging us to make the effort to fulfill our potential. She reminds us that even in an "ordinary" life we are called to share in God's own wisdom and creativity, God's own power and holiness.

For Reflection

- *Ask yourself: How much do I want to be holy and for what reason? What does holiness mean to me? Am I willing to seek out the means? If not, do I want to ask for the grace to do so? (Be honest with yourself.)*

- *Choose one or two areas where you know you often fail. Devise a strategy to help you cope with the problem. Choose a biblical text to refocus your efforts and give you encouragement when you fail.*

- *In your imagination, see yourself helping a troublesome relative or neighbor. Realize that Jesus wants to be present in you to that person, showing them how loved and precious they are to him. Ask him to fill you with his life and love, enabling you to communicate these to all you meet in your daily life.*

- *"Effort means more to God than victory." In which areas do you need to make special effort? Ask Therese to share with you some of her courage and creativity in facing problems.*

Closing Prayer

O Jesus,
it is easy to be discouraged
when I strive for holiness
but don't seem to get very far.

Let me rely on you
and not on my own feeble powers.

Your life seemed a failure
but you went on loving us to the end,
and that's the way you want us
to love one another.

You know my weakness and my sinfulness;
heal the depths I cannot reach,
and transform my violence into gentleness,
my fear into confidence,
my anger into patient love.

Lord Jesus Christ,
set me in your radiance;
fill me with your Spirit;
purify my heart. Amen.

O my God, I desire to love you and to make you loved.
I desire to accomplish your will perfectly.
I desire, in a word, to be a saint.
But I feel my helplessness
and I beg you, O my God,
to be yourself my sanctity.—Therese

Notes

[1] See Judith 9:11.

[2] *Autobiography*, Chapter XV.

[3] Ibid.

[4] Ibid.

[5] Ibid.

[6] *Poems.*

[7] Ibid.

[8] Esther 14:3b, 12a, 19.

[9] Judith 9:9b, 11.

[10] *Autobiography*, Chapter XXXIV.

[11] See John 15:12.

[12] *Autobiography*, Chapter XXXIV.

[13] Ibid.

[14] 1 John 3:18.

[15] *Autobiography*, Chapter XXXIV.

[16] *Autobiography*, Chapter XXXVI.

[17] Ibid. Chapter XXXVIII.

[18] Luke 11:9b-10.

[19] Stephen R. Covey, *The Seven Habits of Highly Effective People: Restoring the Character Ethic* (Simon & Schuster, 1989).

[20] L. Lavelle, *The Meaning of Holiness*, trans. D. O'Sullivan (Catholic Book Club, 1951), p. 7.

[21] Luke 22:42c.

DAY FOUR
Focus on Jesus

Coming Together in the Spirit

Therese comes into the room today carrying a small blue-covered book and a big brown envelope. She sits down purposefully, looking as if she has something to tell us, something to do with the two things she is holding. She speaks.

"Yesterday we were thinking about having courage to do battle with our selfishness so we could be free. But why? Just because we want to be holy? If that alone had been my aim I'd have lost heart absolutely ages ago!

"You see, I knew I had faults and weaknesses like everyone else. I had often been vain, self-pitying and strong-willed. I knew well enough I wasn't perfect. In fact I didn't want to be 'perfect' because that would turn people away from holiness altogether.

"What helped me sustain my efforts wasn't the thought of becoming a 'perfect Therese' but of becoming more Christlike, more like the one I loved.

"If we love we are more ready to do difficult things. A mother who loves will spend hours helping her handicapped child. A husband will watch patiently beside a dying wife day in and day out. A man and a woman who are in love aren't put off by obstacles to their marriage; they surmount them all.

"That's the point of the two things I've brought along today. First is this little book: *The Small Miracle*, by Paul Gallico. It tells the story of Pepino, a young orphan of Assisi, whose beloved donkey, Violetta, is sick.

"Poor Pepino! Violetta is his only friend, the one he loves most, and it seems the doctor can do nothing for her. Pepino is convinced that if he can get Violetta into the crypt where Saint Francis is buried, the saint will cure her. But the entrance is blocked and inaccessible to animals.

"Pepino loved Violetta and so would do anything to make her get better. Like me getting permission to enter Carmel, Pepino goes to the bishop and even, by a miracle, to the pope himself. He just won't take no for an answer. At last, armed with the necessary documents, his goal can be realized. The wall is knocked down and Pepino and Violetta walk into the crypt together. Love surmounts all obstacles.

"Secondly, in this envelope is a picture that I keep before me to remind me continually of whom I love, whom I want to please. I'll show it to you now. It's a picture of the suffering face of Jesus."

Defining Our Thematic Context

Today's theme focuses on Jesus, trying to grow in love of him, making him our life. And with Therese we will do this through gazing on his holy face.

Legend tells us that on the way to Calvary a woman came forward to wipe the sweat and blood from the face of Jesus as he struggled beneath the cross. Afterward, she discovered that he had left the imprint of his features on the cloth she had used.

This cloth became known as the veil of Veronica

(*Veronica* is taken from two Latin words—*vera* and *icon*—meaning "true image"). Therese had a picture of it before her always during prayer time. It reminded her not only of Jesus, but also of her father, whose face had likewise become a suffering face, hidden away in a mental institution without beauty or majesty, like the Lord's face during the time of his passion.

Therese realized that many loved Jesus so long as he gave them good things, healed them, consoled them and made life all sunshine. But fewer would sustain their commitment when he seemed absent, when they had to suffer pain or family tragedy.

At the time of her father's illness Therese encouraged Celine not to draw back from the cup of suffering. Celine should retain her inward peace by contemplating the suffering Christ. *"Jesus burns with love for us—look at his wounds. Look Jesus in the face. There you will see how he loves us."*[1]

Today we will do just that.

Opening Prayer

My God,
Therese wants to share with me
the love she had for your son Jesus,
as she gazed upon the image of his face.

Let this day of retreat be a time
when I contemplate that face with her,
and learn from him in his suffering
more about the meaning of holiness,
a holiness hidden from human eyes
but alight with inner splendor.

Form me in his likeness

that with Therese
I may be a witness to gospel joy
in a world of fragile peace and broken promises.

And I ask this in Jesus' name. Amen.

Retreat Session Four
The Face of Jesus

This fourth day is the central one, the pivot of our retreat. Love of Jesus is the key to understanding Therese.

A saint is an extravagant lover of God. This is what is so attractive about Therese. She is a fulfilled woman because she is a loving person. And her womanhood is generative, life-giving. She wants to share these insights because she wants us too to experience love, freedom, joy, peace—even in the midst of trials and sufferings. She wants us to know the love of Jesus as she does.

In your imagination, join Therese in her room, her "cell," in Carmel. She is sitting back on her heels as Carmelites do because there is no chair. Her room is very plain. There is a plank bed with a straw mattress covered with a dark brown coverlet, a small table with an hourglass and a writing case. On the wall is a large black cross without a corpus. The Carmelite nun is herself supposed to take the place of the crucified. That is her vocation. That is her joy.

The Carmelite Rule enjoins prayer in solitude. Therese therefore is used to being alone but not lonely. Through the open window she hears the song of a bird and catches a glimpse of the creamy candle-like blossoms of the chestnut trees, glowing as if burning in silent adoration.

She has recently received news from her sister Celine, who has visited their father in Caen. The letter lies open beside her.

Before her eyes Therese has placed a picture of the holy face of Jesus in his passion. She calls our attention to it with the words of Scripture: "No one has ever seen God. It is God the only Son, who is close to the Father's heart, who has made him known."[2]

Therese Speaks

This is the picture of Jesus that I love best. I can look at his face for hours, just as you might look at a photograph of someone you love and want to remember continually. And I'll tell you why.

In the Old Testament the face of God was considered sacred. It revealed God's identity, just as each person's face is totally unique. Even identical twins aren't exactly alike. Only you have your face and people recognize you by it. But God is not "one of us" and so doesn't show a face in the Old Testament even to the best of friends.

In Exodus 33 God claims to be a gracious and merciful God. "But," God tells Moses, "you cannot see my face; for no one shall see me and live." Instead, God says to Moses:

> See, there is a place by me where you shall stand in the rock; and while my glory passes by I will put you in a cleft of the rock, and I will cover you with my hand until I have passed by; then I will take away my hand, and you shall see my back; but my face shall not be seen.[3]

Even so, some of God's glory seems to have been reflected in the countenance of Moses, for as he comes down from the mountain his face is shining. Closeness to God has affected Moses' own face.

Because God was a hidden, mysterious God, to seek his face meant to seek God in his deepest reality. It was that for which Israel longed.

> "Come," my heart says, "seek his face!"
>   Your face, LORD, do I seek,
>   Do not hide your face from me.[4]

> Let your face shine upon your servant;
>   save me in your steadfast love.[5]

The face of God lighted Israel's way on earth even in darkness. But God showed us no human face until the Incarnation. Jesus is the human face of God.

> For it is the God who said, "Let light shine out of darkness," who has shone in our hearts to give the light of knowledge of the glory of God in the face of Christ.[6]

Jesus shows us what God is really like. How often the Gospels speak of the look of Jesus—a look of love, a look of compassion, a look of sorrow, of tears, of tenderness, of anger.

Above all there is the face of Jesus as it must have been seen in his passion. That is what I have been attracted to. Stay with me now as I contemplate one of my favorite Gospel scenes. It is the one where the woman of Samaria approaches Jesus. You can read the whole story in the fourth chapter of Saint John's Gospel.

Jesus is sitting by the well of Sichar. (In the ancient Near East, wells were often meeting places for lovers.) Jesus' disciples have gone off to the town to buy food, but he is too weary to accompany them. He sits in the shadow of the well's stone canopy, his eyes sweeping over Mount Gerizim and its rival temple.

Then Jesus sees a woman approach. It is midday, the sixth hour, when no respectable woman would be abroad. This one is obviously avoiding the company of others. She stares openly at the stranger.

Jesus returns her look with one of love and compassion. She is another human being, not an enemy. Then he asks for a drink. He holds out his hands like a beggar. But what does he really want?

In saying, "Give me to drink," it is the love of this poor creature that the Creator of the universe is asking for. He thirsts for love.

I realize that Jesus is now more thirsty than ever, for he meets with nothing but ingratitude and indifference from the disciples of this world. And even among his own disciples, how few hearts he finds that are given to him without reserve, able to experience all the tenderness of his infinite love![7]

Yes, when I see the Samaritan woman and Jesus, when I listen to their conversation as Jesus promises to give her living water, I understand that what he really wants, indeed the only thing he wants, is our love, in return for the gift of his love.

And Jesus proves his love at another "sixth hour" when I see him nailed fast to the cross. He is thirsty again and his whole body cries out for a drink.

His face is bruised and bleeding, the lips swollen and cracked. The crown of thorns presses into his brow and he thirsts not just for water but for recognition and love. He is the Innocent One suffering for the world's salvation.

Yet in his agony he has been left alone. That is why I want to be with him. I want to let him share with me all the love he feels for the human race even when it has rejected him. I don't want to be with him only when he is healing or giving gifts or showing his divine power. I want to be with him for himself alone.

My love for the face of Jesus isn't a morbid fascination. I remember that on Mount Tabor Jesus allowed his chosen disciples to see his face shining and his clothing a brilliant white. Like Moses on the mountain, his closeness to his Father suddenly shone through his ordinary exterior.

But the only words the disciples heard on that occasion were these: "This is my Son the Beloved; listen to him!" Then the glory faded and "they saw no one with them any more, but only Jesus."[8]

The disciples left Jesus when he was suffering, but I want to stay with him, to recognize him, to see "only Jesus" under all the dirt and blood and bruises. I don't want to remain with him only when he is radiant and beautiful.

Real love is like that. For example, when a man named Archie Hill married a woman who already had a son, Barry, needing constant care because of handicaps, Archie grew to understand that love gives even when there seems to be no return. Archie's wife gave herself unstintingly to Barry because she saw the fine, innocent person he was. Others didn't see it. They shunned him.

Then Barry developed cancer and died, nursed lovingly to the end by his mother. Her face now is changed by care and grief, but Archie still loves his wife:

> ...so beautiful when I met her, so lovely, so full of
> pure life.
> Faded now and tired, a tired monument to
> sacrifice.[9]

Real love does not change when people age or are in sorrow. It penetrates below the surface to discover the beauty that is unchangeable.

Jesus loved us to the end. I want to demonstrate that my love given in return doesn't rest upon his giving me good things. I think of him in his agony, when his love was scorned and rejected, and I want to be with him.

My own father's face, the face I had loved more than any other on earth, became a mask that could give me no response. I saw Jesus present in my mentally ill father, numbered among the poor, the despised, the rejected.

For Jesus is present among those scorned and forgotten. He is with those who bear mental handicaps, made to feel useless and a burden on society. He is with the business manager who defrauds his company and is shamed before his wife and family. He is with the person you marginalize through your own prejudice and exclude from your friendship.

I wanted to recognize Jesus in all these people and love him for himself no matter what his disguise. I wrote him this prayer:

> *O consider this*
> *that your divine face*
> *was unknown even to your kindred.*
> *But you left us your image so still and bright*
> *And Lord, you know I recognized you.*
> *Through the tear-stained veil, Face of the Eternal One,*
> *I saw you radiant.*
> *How your veiled countenance*
> *comforts and delights my heart.*
> *O consider this.*[10]

Call to Prayer

Therese now invites us to pray with her, using one of

her favorite Scripture passages and a response written by herself on the back of a picture of the crucifixion.

Have before you a picture of the face of Christ such as that from the Shroud of Turin. Or hold a crucifix and concentrate on the face. It may help to light a candle or burn incense.

Begin by playing some music, possibly part of the Passion sequence from Handel's *Messiah*. Then either listen to Therese reading or, if you are praying in a group, have one person read the Isaiah passages while the rest join in the response.

> The Lord GOD has given me
>   the tongue of a teacher,
> that I may know how to sustain
>   the weary with a word.
> Morning by morning he wakens—
>   wakens my ear
>   to listen as those who are taught.[11]

Response: *O Lord, you know that I love you.*
But have mercy on me, for I am a sinner.

> The Lord GOD has opened my ear,
>   and I was not rebellious,
>   I did not turn backward.
> I gave my back to those who struck me,
>   and my cheeks to those who pulled out the beard;
> I did not hide my face
>   from insult and spitting.[12]

R. *O Lord, you know that I love you.*
But have mercy on me, for I am a sinner.

> Who has believed what we have heard?
>   And to whom has the arm of the LORD been
>   revealed?

For he grew up before him like a young plant
and like a root out of dry ground....[13]

R. *O Lord, you know that I love you.*
But have mercy on me, for I am a sinner.

...he had no form or majesty that we should look on
him,
nothing in his appearance that we should desire
him.
He was despised and rejected by others,
a man of suffering and acquainted with infirmity;
and as one from whom others hide their faces,
he was despised and we held him of no account.[14]

R. *O Lord, you know that I love you.*
But have mercy on me, for I am a sinner.

Surely he has borne our infirmities
and carried our diseases;
yet we accounted him stricken,
cut down by God and afflicted.
But he was wounded for our transgressions,
crushed for our iniquities....[15]

R. *O Lord, you know that I love you.*
But have mercy on me, for I am a sinner.

...upon him was the punishment that made us
whole
and by his bruises we are healed.
All we like sheep have gone astray,
we have all turned to our own way,
and the LORD has laid on him the iniquity of us all.[16]

R. *O Lord, you know that I love you.*
But have mercy on me, for I am a sinner.

He was oppressed, and he was afflicted,

yet he did not open his mouth;
like a lamb that is led to the slaughter,
and like a sheep before its shearers is silent,
so he did not open his mouth.[17]

R. *O Lord, you know that I love you.*
But have mercy on me, for I am a sinner.

Yet it was the will of the LORD to crush him with
pain.
...[T]hrough him the will of the LORD shall prosper.
Out of his anguish he shall see light;
...The righteous one, my servant, shall make many
righteous,
and he shall bear their iniquities.[18]

R. *O Lord, you know that I love you.*
But have mercy on me, for I am a sinner.

Therefore I will allot him a portion with the great,
and he shall divide the spoil with the strong;
because he poured himself out to death,
and was numbered with the transgressors;
yet he bore the sin of many
and made intercession for the transgressors.[19]

R. *O Lord, you know that I love you.*
But have mercy on me, for I am a sinner.

A Call to Love

Therese's love for Jesus was characterized by a great
tenderness even in her early youth. At the time of her
First Communion she could say that *"we had exchanged*
looks, he and I, insignificant though I was, and we had
understood one another."[20] But Communion was more than

a look—it was fusion. Henceforth Therese longed for the sacramental presence which would make her one flesh with Christ. This became a reality as she lived continually with the gaze of Jesus upon her: he looking at her, she looking at him. As people who have lived with one another over many years can take on something even of physical likeness, so Therese wished to become a living icon of the Lord.

During her meditation periods in Carmel, one hour every morning and evening, Therese kept a picture of the face of Jesus always before her; one marked her breviary, and in her last illness the same picture was pinned to her bed curtains in the infirmary to help her bear the pain.

Therese saw in the face of Jesus the most personal manifestation of his individuality. While the symbol of the heart is universal, the face is always particular. It is the "external heart." Here on earth we "make our face" (but not our features) by the way we live. The thoughts within affect our outward expression.

> The heart changes the countenance
>   either for good or for evil.
> The sign of a happy heart is a cheerful face....[21]

Therese advised her novices always to keep a peaceful expression on their faces, like that of a contented child who knows she will be cared for by a loving parent. Hardness and inner anxiety leave their mark, whereas peace is born of wisdom and acceptance of life as it is. For:

> Wisdom makes one's face shine
> and the hardness of one's countenance is changed.[22]

In the Gospels Therese hoped to glimpse the reality of

Jesus as in a mirror, who he really was—and is. With John of the Cross, she could say of the Scripture:

O crystal spring
If only in your mirror-face
You would suddenly form
The eyes I have desired
Which I bear imprinted deep in my heart.[23]

Living a continual search for Jesus, keeping his face before her, allowing his words and actions to inspire her, Therese's one desire was to mirror Christ. The photographs we have of Therese do not depict a sweet girl but a woman who is dedicated and mature—like a female Christ.

As she venerated the suffering face, Therese realized that Jesus' features will not become ours unless, like him, we learn to recognize and welcome his presence in what is, humanly speaking, unlovely. Nearly always the holy face is disfigured, marred by human hands, hence the need to accept God in the hard and painful events that befall us. *"Jesus has sent us the best chosen cross that he could devise in his immense love.... How can we complain when he himself was considered 'as one struck by God and afflicted'?"*[24] Therese wrote to Celine at the time of their father's illness.

It is only by learning to recognize the face of Jesus in his sufferings that we can one day know him in his glory:

I suffer, but the hope of the homeland gives me courage. Soon we shall be in heaven.... There will be neither day nor night any more, but the Face of Jesus will bathe all in light like no other.[25]

Love wishes to share all. As Jesus was often hidden and

unrecognized, Therese sought a similar hiddenness. She desired to please only the Beloved, not self.

> *He, the King of Kings, humbled himself in such a manner that his countenance was hidden and no one recognized him.... And I too want to hide my face, I want my Beloved alone to see it.*[26]

The hiddenness Therese speaks of is not physical enclosure, it is the secret relationship with Jesus that is devoid of self-importance, self-display or self-pity.

Our faces, and those of others, are marred by sin. We can still pray with Therese, however, that the divine image will shine through all our brokenness so that we become "other Christs."

The Transfiguration reminds us that the victory of Christ shone through his passion; it will shine in our lives, too. But the cost is heavy if we want the prize. The glory fades and the disciples see no one but Jesus. So it must be with us.

> Blest are those captivated by your face, Jesus Lord,
> And who through your love
> Have recognized everywhere the seal of your image.
>
> Blest are those whom your presence has despoiled;
> You invaded them; seized by you,
> All their life has become transparent,
> Letting you be seen.
>
> Living icons where your mystery
> has appeared on our paths:
> Blest are they who in your hands
> pass out of this world to the Father.[27]

For Reflection

- *Light a candle and ponder silently these words from Scripture:*

  For we do not proclaim ourselves; we proclaim Jesus Christ as Lord and ourselves as your slaves for Jesus' sake. For it is the God who said, "Let light shine out of darkness," who has shone in our hearts to give the light of the knowledge of the glory of God in the face of Christ.[28]

- *Resolve to read the Gospels regularly and systematically. Will you set a time for this daily? Weekly? Monthly?*

- *Find a picture of the face of Christ such as that from the Shroud of Turin. Let it speak to you of the Passion and the meaning of God's love. Look at it frequently during the day.*

- *Think of someone in whom you find it difficult to recognize Christ, someone who is for you "without beauty, without majesty." See yourself being a "Veronica"—offering love, compassion, understanding, even in a small way. Reflect that in doing this you are reflecting Christ and allowing his image to be imprinted on your own heart.*

Closing Prayer

Jesus,
I ask you for the grace to recognize you most
    especially
in the mystery of your suffering face.

Help me to realize that holiness
is about becoming like you,
finding you here and now
in much that is unlovely, painful and sorrowful.

Holiness is not about being perfect and beautiful;
it is about being myself in all my weakness and
   vulnerability
and still discovering that you are here with me,
loving me as I am.

You know from experience what it is to be human
in a fallen and sinful world
that thirsts for love, a love only you can give.

Jesus,
I don't want to seek anything for myself.
Rather, I want you to be the center of my life.

I want to accept you however you come to me.
Let me see your face.
Let me hear your voice in all that happens.

Truly you are enough for me.
Amen.

Father as you have loved me
to the point of giving me
your only Son to be my Savior,
I beg you to look upon me
only through the face of Jesus
and in his heart, on fire with love.—Therese

Notes

1 "Letter LXIII," April 4, 1889.
2 John 1:18.
3 Exodus 33:21-23.
4 Psalm 27:8-9.
5 Psalm 31:16.

[6] 2 Corinthians 4:6.

[7] "Letter to Marie."

[8] Mark 9:7, 8b.

[9] Archie Hill, *Closed World of Love* (Shepherd and Walwyn Ltd., 1963), p. 98.

[10] *Poems.*

[11] Isaiah 50:4.

[12] Isaiah 50:5-6.

[13] Isaiah 53:1-2.

[14] Isaiah 53:2-3.

[15] Isaiah 53:4-5.

[16] Isaiah 53:5-6.

[17] Isaiah 53:7.

[18] Isaiah 53:10-11.

[19] Isaiah 53:12.

[20] *Autobiography*, Chapter XII.

[21] Sirach 13:25-26a.

[22] Ecclesiastes 8:1b.

[23] John of the Cross, Spiritual Canticle XI.

[24] "Letter LXXXVIII," July 18, 1890.

[25] "Letter LXXXIV."

[26] "Letter CXXVI," August 13, 1893.

[27] *Latroun Abbey*, trans. the Carmelites of Terre Haute, Indiana. Used with permission.

[27] 2 Corinthians 4:5-6.

DAY FIVE
To Love Is to Act

Coming Together in the Spirit

As Therese focused on the face of Jesus, as symbol of his person, and grew in her love for him, so she desired to show her love more and more.

In a scene from the musical *Fiddler on the Roof* Tevye, the Russian Jewish milkman, muses on the whole new world that is opening up. His daughters, one after the other, choose to marry for "love" rather than accept a marriage arranged by their parents. That wasn't part of the understanding when Tevye married his own wife, Golde. Now, after twenty-five years, he decides to ask her whether or not she loves him. It never occurred to him before!

In a sung dialogue between Tevye and Golde, Golde tries to make up her mind—does she or does she not love her husband? To her it seems irrelevant, something not included in their original marriage contract. But Tevye insists. At last Golde concedes the point—she supposes she must love him. For twenty-five years she has worked for him, cooked for him, borne his children, shared his bed. If that isn't love, what is? And she's right! We can't help but agree.

So would Eliza Doolittle, who sings in *My Fair Lady*:

Don't talk of stars burning above
if you're in love, show me.

Too much talk and no action will not convince anyone.
Deeds, even if the words of love are absent, are ultimately
what count. As Scripture says, "Above all, maintain
constant love for one another, for love covers a multitude
of sins."[1]

As Therese leans forward to speak, we catch sight of
some small booklets pinned over her heart. She realizes
we have noticed them and she unpins them from her
habit to show them to us. She has been wearing a little
copy of each of the Gospels—Matthew, Mark, Luke and
John.

"I have these with me always," she says, "and I always
recommend that my friends have copies like this about
their persons as well. Any spare moment that comes my
way I read some words of Jesus and think how best I can
put them into action."

Defining Our Thematic Context

When Therese looked at the suffering face of Jesus she
saw the portrait of the one she loved. But contemplating
Jesus did not evoke protestations of love, tears over the
passion, sentimental longings. During her final illness,
Therese asked: "What is the good of writing beautiful
things about suffering? It means nothing, nothing! When
you're going through it, then you know the
worthlessness of all this eloquence."

Contemplating Jesus energized Therese to do
whatever she could to become more Christlike. That
meant discovering the sort of person Jesus was, full of
strength and compassion, ready to put others before self,

ready to take a courageous stand for truth, not giving in to self-pity when life was hard.

As Jesus was always doing the Father's will, so Therese wanted her actions to be motivated by his prayer, "Thy will be done." She didn't take the easy way out, waiting for other people to tell her what to do. She allowed herself to be challenged personally by the Gospels. She found in them wisdom that affected her way of living, right down to the nitty-gritty of daily life and relationships.

Holiness depends upon our resolution to become Christlike. This is what we are considering in more detail today.

Opening Prayer

Heavenly Father,
Jesus' only desire on earth
was that your kingdom should come,
your will be done.

Help me to hallow your name by becoming holy
    myself,
sharing in the holiness of Jesus.
Holiness is grounded in doing your will
in all the circumstances of my life
whatever they may be.

Help me to be radical in my following of Jesus,
not content with only second-best, a lukewarm love.
Real love doesn't stop and say,
"Enough, Lord, I have given you enough."

Love is always reaching out, growing stronger,
finding new ways to express itself.

I ask for the gift of a love like that of Therese,
always finding new applications in reality.

And I ask this in Jesus' name. Amen.

RETREAT SESSION FIVE

Love in Action

One image that Therese was especially fond of she
acted out in a kind of parable.

Let us look at her now as she comes down the cloister,
walking with a firm step. As usual, she wears a thick
brown habit, well patched and darned. It is dusk. The air
is balmy and the first stars are coming out in the
purple-shot sky. In the distance we can hear strains of
chamber music: An elegant drawing room in Lisieux has
guests for a soiree.

In the Carmel the only sound is that of the nuns in
their soft rope-soled slippers. It is the time of the evening
silence. Work is finished for the day and the sisters have
some free time to spend alone as they wish.

The cloister garden forms an open space in the center
of the convent buildings. In the middle of it is a fine stone
crucifix. Therese was photographed here as a novice
when she first received the habit a few days after her
sixteenth birthday. What memories it holds of her
growing years! The garden around the crucifix is grassy
with a few shrubs and rose bushes. Therese is alone,
enjoying the quiet peace and lengthening shadows. She
leans forward among the rose plants, reaching for a few
blooms. She cuts the roses expertly, ignoring the thorns
that tear her hands and leave a tiny smear of blood

along her wrist.

Then she approaches the tall crucifix and wordlessly unpetals each flower. The soft petals fall over the feet of the corpus and are blown about by the breeze until they disappear. She does nothing to gather them up. She just turns and walks back to the cloister and up to her bare room.

Therese Speaks

You'll often see pictures or statues of me carrying roses. These images are rather sentimental and out of fashion now, but they say something about what I mean by really loving God in action.

Even when I was dying and had energy for nothing else I used to scatter flower petals over the crucifix lying on my bed cover. It was the only way left for me to express my love by doing something concrete.

Scattering flowers is a symbol of how I see my life. You'll notice that I pick flowers only to unpetal them. That leaves me empty-handed. Look—I've got nothing in my hands, nothing at all. Everything is given.

My life's task is simply to scatter flowers, to make gestures of love that are within everyone's reach. I'm not called to work among the lepers of Molokai like Father Damien. I can't travel to foreign lands and preach the gospel like my two priest friends in the missions. I don't even have the stamina that some of you need to care for a sick relative or raise several children.

All I have to give God are the thousand and one "nothings" that make up my day: the opportunity to lend a hand to a sister in need, to do another person a kindness, to restrain a hurtful remark, to pray when I don't feel like praying. It's easy to overlook these tiny things, to think they aren't worth offering to God. But most of us don't have anything else.

Think for a moment of your own life and the opportunities it offers: the possibility of taking a deprived child out for a treat with your own children, of writing a letter for someone who is blind, of visiting someone in the hospital even though you have a busy schedule, of inviting a lonely neighbor for coffee and a chat. Holiness is made up of small things like this done for God and done with love.

I have no other way to prove my love than "scattering flowers," that is, not letting slip any little sacrifice, any look or word, but profiting by the least thing and doing it for love.

I want to suffer for love, enjoy for love, and so scatter flowers before God. I won't leave even one flower unpetalled. And while scattering I want to sing—even if I have to gather my flowers from among thorns. And my song shall be all the more tuneful if the thorns are long and sharp.

I can't do outstanding things like preaching the gospel or shedding my blood. But what does that matter? Other family members are at work while I, like a small child, stay close to my parents and give them joy.[2]

You see, I let myself be pulled to pieces like the roses just in order to give God pleasure. I'm not looking for any other reward.

People sometimes think my life in Carmel is heroic, but it isn't. It's ordinary, like yours. It's full of the trifling actions and encounters that fill everyone's hours.

I've had trials too. The painful separation from my parents, depression and thoughts of suicide, enduring severe cold, the lack of youthful freedom. But these are no more or less than the sorrows each one has to cope with as part of life. Nobody is without suffering.

Whatever happens I just cast myself before God, forget myself, like a fallen flower placed before Jesus to give him pleasure. In one of my poems I wrote of myself as a rose, its petals scattered every which way, not some beautiful bloom adorning an altar.

> *This fallen rose*
> *is a true image of that heart*
> *which makes a whole burnt sacrifice*
> *of every moment, every part....*
> *For love of loveliness supreme,*
> *dying to cast myself away*
> *were bright fulfillment of my dream,*
> *I'd prove my love no easier way.*[3]

A sister in another convent read this poem and suggested that I should add another verse intimating that in heaven God would gather up the petals and fashion a wondrous flower from them. But I wouldn't go along with that idea at all. I was irrevocably plucked and scattered, each instant a "whole burnt sacrifice." Why try to imagine some other finale?

As far as I'm concerned I'm not looking for any return except to please the One I love. Holiness can't be hoarded or held on to any more than love can. You've got to be giving it away all the time.

Michelangelo says that "trifles make perfection and perfection is no trifle." He fashioned his wonderful sculptures chip by chip, each part incorporated into a perfect whole, making use of faults in the marble to find an even better pattern. So I find holiness in everything, love in everything, God in everything. But it doesn't happen all in a day.

Now I want to come back to that copy of the Gospels I showed you and which I wear continually over my heart. How do you think I find ways to please God in my circumscribed life? I'm not up to a lot of fasting, heavy work, night-long vigils; nor am I involved in social or political action on behalf of the oppressed.

So what can I do? Here's my secret. I read and reread the Gospels so as to discover moment by moment how to please Jesus in my own life, how to act as he wants me to act. I don't rely on others to tell me what to do. I ponder his words myself, and apply them to the practical details of daily living.

I'm like a child who knows she can't buy a grand gift for her parents. So she colors a card for them, or picks a few wildflowers to show her love and her desire to please them. And this gives them as much or more pleasure than if she borrows money and buys them something that looks grander but contains less of herself.

Keeping the fire of love going means adding pieces of wood, sticks and even straw. *When we are in darkness, in dryness, then there is no wood within our reach, but surely we can throw little bits of straw on the fire.... I have tried it. When I feel nothing, when I am incapable of praying or of practicing virtue, then is the moment to look for small occasions, "nothings," that give Jesus more pleasure than the empire of the world, more even than martyrdom generously suffered. For example—a smile, a friendly word, when I would much prefer to say nothing or look bored, etc.*[4] You can make your own application.

Now I'll share with you some Gospel passages that I made my own and you can consider how to apply them in your own life.

"Do not judge, so that you may not be judged" (Matthew 7:1). *How do I react when I want to fix my mind's eye on the defects of some sister who hasn't much attraction for me? I remind myself in a great hurry of all that sister's good qualities, all her good intentions. True enough, she has made a slip this time; but who's going to tell us how often she has fought temptation and conquered it, only she was too humble to* let us notice it? It's even possible that what I think of as a fault was in reality a praiseworthy act. And what is the best way to ensure that God will judge you favorably or rather, won't judge you at all? Why, I do my best to have none but charitable thoughts in my own mind at all times.[5]

"If you love those who love you, what credit is that to you? For even sinners love those who love them" (Luke 6:32). Of course, you don't meet enemies in Carmel; but when all is said and done you have your sympathies. One sister attracts you; another sister—well, you would go a good long way 'round to avoid meeting her; without knowing it she is "persecutress." Good, then Jesus tells me this is the sister I've got to love, the sister I've got to pray for. And just loving her isn't enough; you've got to prove it. We find a natural satisfaction in making presents, especially if they are surprise presents, to people we are fond of, but that's not charity—sinners find the same.[6]

"Give to everyone who begs from you, and do not refuse anyone who wants to borrow from you" (Matthew 5:42). Giving what one's asked for—how much less enjoyable than offering something of one's own accord, out of the goodness of one's heart. Moreover, people have different ways of asking. If they do it nicely the gift doesn't cost you much, but if they don't succeed in wording the request so tactfully, your pride is up in arms at once. Unless your soul is well grounded in charity, you hit upon a thousand reasons for refusing altogether. First of all you have to impress on the wretched woman a sense of her great tactlessness, and only after that do you do what she asks as a special favor—probably some tiny service which wouldn't have taken a twentieth of the time you spent airing your imaginary grievance.

And when it comes to letting people take away what belongs to you without asking to have it back—that's much harder than giving things to people who ask for them.

Oh, what peace comes flooding into the soul when once it

learns to rise above its natural sensitiveness.[7]

"And if anyone wants to sue you and take your coat, give your cloak as well..." (Matthew 5:40). *I suppose the idea of giving up one's cloak is renouncing the last shred of dignity, treating oneself as everyone's drudge, everyone's slave. Well, now that you've taken off your coat, you're in a good position for walking—running if you want to. When I do a service to other people, they ought to get the impression that I'm grateful and honored to have the opportunity; when they take away something that I'm wanting to use, there must be no show of reluctance; I must look as though I were glad to be rid of it. Of course, when I tell you these ideas I don't mean for a moment that I carry them out. But somehow I get peace even from wanting to carry them out.*[8]

"But when you give a banquet, invite the poor, the crippled, the lame, and the blind" (Luke 14:13). *People who suffer from imperfections get left out of things. I'm thinking of faults such as want of judgment, want of education, the touchiness you find in certain people's characters that spoil the amenities of life. It's true, moral disabilities of this kind are chronic, there's no real hope of curing them...but often just a word or a friendly smile are enough to make these difficult natures open out.*

The only feast a Carmelite nun can give to all her sisters is a feast made up of kindness and gaiety.... It's the cheerful giver God loves.[9]

"This is my commandment, that you love one another as I have loved you" (John 15:12). *Meditating on these words of Jesus, I began to see how imperfect my own love was; it was so obvious that I didn't love my sisters as God loves them. I realize now that perfect love means putting up with other people's shortcomings, feeling no surprise at their weaknesses, finding encouragement at even the slightest evidence of good qualities in them.... Always, when I act as charity bids, I have this feeling that it is Jesus acting in me. The closer my union with him, the greater my love for all the sisters without distinction.*[10]

As I've said, it's not a question of always succeeding in loving others and reaching out to them. What matters is continually trying and trusting in God's grace to help us get up when we fall.

A Call to Love

We are what we do. As psychologist C. J. Jung observes: "Our personality develops in the course of our life from germs that are hard or impossible to discern, and it is only our deeds that reveal who we are."[11]

In this statement we are not looking at the perennial question—which is more important, being or doing? To that we all know the "correct" answer; for "doing" in that context refers to our job, employment, as if our person could be defined by our persona—as teacher, nurse, miner, clerk and so on. When our job terminates, are we a nobody? Rather, Jung states what is much more relevant— our deeds reveal what kind of person we really are. Being and doing are not at variance in a person of integrity.

For example, reading books on prayer, talking a lot about God and giving lectures on how to pray does not make someone a prayerful person. Only those who actually pray will become persons of prayer. In the same way, one kind deed is worth more than a thousand words on the importance of helping others.

Saint Teresa of Avila, reformer of the Carmelites, laid great stress on the practical love of others. She was fond of pointing out that we can never be sure that we love God, although there may be good reason for thinking that we do; but we can never be in doubt about whether or not we love our neighbor. If we concentrate on the latter we will not go astray for, as she says in her book, *Interior Castle*, "be sure that in proportion that you advance in sisterly charity you are increasing in the love of God."

To call Therese the "Little Flower" is misleading. Little flower? Rather, "little bar of steel!" But so tenderly, so silently was Therese sacrificed that the pain, the anguish, the effort are even now overlooked. The joy of giving is ultimately all that matters, all that remains.

Therese would heartily agree with this view of sanctity:

> Why were the saints saints?
> Because they were cheerful when it was difficult to
>   be patient,
> and because they pushed on when they wanted to
>   stand still,
> and kept silent when they wanted to talk,
>   and were agreeable when they wanted to be
>   disagreeable.
> That was all.
> It was quite simple and always will be.

Simple, yes; easy, no. But when we have done what we can, put our little sticks on the fire of love, let our insignificant offerings be tossed away and trampled, then we have no need to worry.

For Reflection

- *Choose one or two of the Gospel passages that inspired Therese and apply them in a specific way to your own life.*

- *Therese liked to scatter flowers. What image of sacrificial love appeals to you? Embody your love for Jesus in some symbolic action: for example, a prostration, holding out empty hands, a mime or dance.*

- *Think of the people who have died but who once showed you love. Imagine them looking at you now and encouraging you to grow in self-acceptance as once they accepted you. Thank God for all those people who have been images of divine love in your life. Resolve to be an image of love for others.*

Closing Prayer

Dear Jesus,
loving our neighbor as ourselves
was the first rule of love revealed in Scripture.
God knew how powerful a motive self-love is
and that there could be no higher standard
by which to measure love of neighbor.

But you, Jesus, gave us a new commandment
calling us not just to love others as we love ourselves
(because often we don't love ourselves enough,
or at least, not in the right way).
Instead you ask us to love others as you love them
and will love them until the end of time.

Jesus, you never tell us to do what is impossible,
and yet you can see even more clearly than I can
how very weak and imperfect I am.

If, then, you tell me to love others as you love them,
it must mean that you want to go on doing this
in and through me;
it wouldn't be possible any other way.

There would be no new commandment
if you hadn't meant to give me the means to keep it,

because I can do nothing of my own accord.

Give me the grace I need
and take possession of my heart in such a way
that you live and move and love in me,

Then others will recognize you present in my
presence
as I recognize you present in them. Amen. (Based on
the words of Therese)

*Lord, in the evening of life, I shall appear before you with
empty hands, for I do not ask you, Lord, to count my
works. I want only you, my Beloved.*—Therese

Notes

1 1 Peter 4:8.
2 "Letter to Marie."
3 *Poems.*
4 "Letter CXXII," July 18, 1893.
5 *Autobiography,* Chapter XXXIV.
6 Ibid., Chapter XXXV.
7 Ibid.
8 Ibid.
9 Ibid., Chapter XXXVIII.
10 Ibid., Chapter XXXIV.
11 *Selected Writings of C.G. Jung,* introduced by Anthony Storr
(Fontana, 1983), p. 196.

Day Six
Love as Vocation

Coming Together in the Spirit

Therese greets us today in the convent garden. Behind her is a grassy field, where she has been making hay with the other sisters, and a pebbled path that leads up to a small shrine of Our Lady set in the wall. Therese points it out and then draws our attention to the fact that a high wall encircles the whole property. Within the confines of this house and garden the nuns must live out the whole of their lives.

"It's strange to think that since I was fifteen I've lived in this small patch of land. No more running in the meadows for me, no more picking wildflowers and seeing vistas reaching into the distance; no variety of towns and shops, no travel to foreign countries. Listen to this story Oscar Wilde tells. I often feel like his 'Happy Prince.'

> There was once a fine statue of a prince erected in a big city. He stood on a high pedestal, unmoving, glittering with precious stones.
> One day a swallow who had missed leaving with its companions at the time of migration took shelter at the statue's feet. After his daily excursions over the city the swallow would bring news to the prince. It was cold, and many poor families were hidden

away in the back streets, unseen by the prince on his pedestal.

The swallow told of a poor seamstress whose children were starving, of an elderly couple freezing in their hovel, of a sick mother whose husband could not afford medicines. Each time the prince, whose hitherto frozen emotions were being touched, gave a jewel from his person, and the swallow would fly off to deliver it where it was most needed.

At last the swallow died, exhausted from work and exposure. By now the prince was no longer a fine bejeweled statue. He was decrepit, denuded of his gems, blind and blackened. When next the mayor and councillors passed by, they decided that the statue should be taken away and replaced by another. The prince was melted down in a furnace. All that was left when the fire had done its work was his heart. The prince had given himself away, but the reality behind his image—his love and generosity—were indestructible.

"I'm like that prince in that I can't go places, but I do have a heart that can love and allow itself to be given for others. I'm here in Carmel, so I have to rely on other people in many ways when it comes to doing good in the wider world.

"I hear of much suffering and need, but I can't always respond with my personal presence. Neither can you, when you hear of distant wars and natural disasters. But ultimately that doesn't matter. We are called to love and to be love in the heart of the Church. Each one of us has a specific task to carry out. Practically speaking, we can only cultivate the small area of responsibility that falls to our care here and now.

"Good deeds pass. What motivates them remains and

forms our person at its core. As Scripture says:

> If I speak in the tongues of mortals and of angels,
> but do not have love, I am a noisy gong or a clanging
> cymbal. And if I have prophetic powers, and
> understand all mysteries and all knowledge, and if I
> have all faith, so as to remove mountains, but do not
> have love, I am nothing. If I give away all my
> possessions, and if I hand over my body so that I
> may boast, but do not have love, I gain nothing.[1]

"If what we do is not done out of love, no matter how grand our actions, they are useless."

Defining Our Thematic Context

Yesterday we looked at the need for love in action—in patience, kindness, nonjudgmentalism. A holy person is one whose love is enfleshed in a thousand acts of neighborly kindness.

Therese had great desires. She wanted to do great things for God, but knew well enough that she hadn't the opportunity to accomplish great deeds. But what she could do was to "be love" in the heart of the Church.

Opening Prayer

My God,
open my eyes, open my heart
so that I may understand the reality of your love for
   me,
and the love you want to receive from me in return.

You are all-merciful.

You understand that I find it hard
really to want to love you
when I experience myself as a sinner, selfish and
self-centered.

Yet you continue to call me;
you want to inflame me with the fire of love
so that others can warm themselves by the light and
   heat
burning within me.

May I want to make my life a life of love, a Christlike
   life:
This is my gift to the world and to the Church.

Show me how,
and may I learn from Therese
that my faults and weaknesses and failures
should never hold me back.

I don't have to earn your love; it is there, waiting,
and all you want is for me to hold out my hands
to receive what you so long to give.

May love light up my mortal frame
so others catch the living flame.

And I ask this in Jesus' name. Amen.

RETREAT SESSION SIX
Being Love in the Heart of the Church

Shortly after her Christmas conversion at age
fourteen, Therese happened to be praying when a holy

picture slipped out of her missal. All that was visible was the wounded and bleeding hand of Christ crucified.

Therese immediately felt drawn to gather up that blood—poured out, wasted, unheeded; and she set herself to pray for a condemned criminal she had heard of, a man named Pranzini, who had committed a brutal murder.

Later Therese read in the newspaper that the unrepentant Pranzini, on his way to the guillotine, had at the last moment asked for the crucifix, cried and kissed it three times. Therese felt confident that she had discovered a new vocation of intercessory prayer.

Therese Speaks

I've never forgotten that incident of my girlhood when I prayed so hard for Pranzini; and indeed all my life I've remembered to pray for him. It was an incident that demonstrated to me the power of prayer. We belong to one another. Nobody whom you pray for and hold up before God is outside the reach of love.

One of the reasons I became a Carmelite was to pray for others. As long as there were men and women who had not heard of God or did not love God, I wanted to be there loving and praying on their behalf.

We need each other. Personal holiness is diffusive. It is a gift to the whole Church. In the same way, personal sin not only damages the individual sinner, it permeates and weakens the whole Body of Christ.

In my early years in Carmel I suffered from loneliness, sorrow, difficulties in adjusting to my new life. But I was spurred on by the thought that others depended on me, on my fidelity and commitment, even though my acts of love were hidden and unknown.

Now I find myself filled with great desires—to be and do everything for Jesus. My love for him has grown so strong. *I want to be a priest, a teacher, a missionary, a martyr, a great saint—and not only one saint but all of them at once. I want to be a Francis of Assisi, a Saint John, Saint Agnes, Saint Joan of Arc and all the rest.*

During prayer these desires made me suffer a veritable martyrdom, so I opened Saint Paul's Letters to look for some answer. My eyes fell on the twelfth and thirteenth chapters of the First Letter to the Corinthians. There I read that not everyone can be apostles, prophets, doctors, etc. The Church is made up of different members and the eye cannot be the hand at the same time.

This was clear enough, but my desire for an answer was still unfulfilled and I could not find peace. Without being discouraged I went on reading and found help in this sentence: "Search eagerly for the more perfect gifts, but I will show you a more excellent way!" And the apostle explains how all the more perfect gifts are nothing without love. LOVE is the EXCELLENT WAY that leads to God. At last I had found rest! Considering the mystical body of the Church I could not recognize myself in any of the members Saint Paul describes, or rather, I wanted to see myself in all of them. It was love that gave me the key to my vocation. I realized that if the Church has a body made up of different members, the most necessary, the most noble of them all, could not be lacking.

I understood that the Church had a heart and that that heart was on fire with love. I understood that only love could make the Church's members act. If love were to grow cold, the apostles would no longer proclaim the gospel, the martyrs would refuse to shed their blood. I understood that all vocations are contained in love—that love is everything—that it embraces all time and all space. In a word, love is eternal.

Then in an excess of delirious joy I cried out: "O Jesus, my Love, I have at last found my vocation. My vocation is love."

Yes, I have found my place in the Church and it is you, O my God, who have given it to me. In the heart of the Church, my mother, I will be love. In that way I will be everything and my dream will come true.

How can one speak of a delirious joy? But that is not the right word. For it was rather the calm and serene peace experienced by the navigator on seeing the lighthouse that will guide him into port. O Shining Light, LOVE, I know how to reach you. I have found the secret of making your flame my own.

Jesus, I know that love can only be repaid by love. Therefore I have sought and found the way to ease my heart—by offering you love for love.[2]

I expressed this to my sister Marie when she asked for a few words from me about the way of love. She misunderstood me, thinking my great desires are a proof of my love. Like her, you may well be feeling that your love wouldn't reach such heights.

If so, then you've certainly misunderstood. *My desires for martyrdom are nothing; it is not they that give me the limitless confidence I feel in my heart.*

What pleases God is to see me love my littleness and poverty, the blind hope I have in his mercy. That is my sole treasure. Why should that treasure not be yours also?

Let us love to feel nothing. Then we shall be poor in spirit and Jesus will come for us, far away as we are, and will transform us in love's flame. How I wish I could make you realize what I mean. It is trust, nothing but trust, that must bring us to love.

I feel that Jesus wants to grant us the same graces, wants to give us his heaven as a free gift.... I am sure that the good God would not give you the desire to be possessed by him, by his merciful love, if he did not have this favor in store for you.[3]

If you have ever been in love, you know what it is like when the person you love does not respond, is unfaithful or behaves as if he or she couldn't care less.

Conversely, if you have discovered that someone loves you, how blessed you feel. Listen to these words of a woman who understands love for love:

> Who does not know the passionate, inarticulate confession of the heart bowed to the dust, abashed and trembling, because it is so utterly unworthy of the love given to it, unworthy of choosing and being chosen by, the friend? Doesn't an undeserved love show up our defects and faults in a light incomparably more glaring than all the reproofs and scorn of our enemies? Oscar Wilde once achieved this happy phrase: "No human being is worthy to receive love. Love is a sacrament we ought only to receive on our knees with 'Lord, I am not worthy' on our lips."[4]

One of the hallmarks of love is that it isn't calculating. I've seen myself as a child before God, and children can give only their love. This is the precious thing their parents want more than anything else.

But in the way I love, I am an adult, extravagant and generous. Because I love Jesus I want to link myself with everyone so as to give them all to him—sinners, unbelievers, the poor, the sick, the destitute, the homeless. They all have a place in my heart. My heart embraces the whole world.

It would be a great pity to make a retreat that ended with the resolve to do only a tiny bit more for God. True, God is always wanting to give the divine self to us; God isn't difficult to please, much less a tyrant or taskmaster. But God does yearn for us to show our love generously; divine love can't be satisfied with what costs less than everything. Indeed, *it belongs to love to sacrifice everything— to give generously, to become spend-thrift, to act with folly.*

Love is prodigal to excess and never counts the cost; love knows not how to calculate and freely foregoes all hope of any dividends. O happy recklessness! O blessed intoxication of love! O for that love that gives all with the total surrender of self besides!

Nevertheless, with many of us, how often it is only after the greatest deliberation that we give way; how loath we are to sacrifice our temporal advantages and our spiritual interests! Does this deserve the name of love? No, for love is blind; it is a raging torrent that sweeps up everything in its train.[5]

God gives us everything and wants everything in return, wants us to live the language of love. For the married person, love of one person means a certain detachment from all others. A husband or wife can't have the same relationship with anyone else who comes along. But if you really love you're happy to make that choice. There's not even the possibility of another course of action because if you love you can do no other.

I choose Jesus. Beside him, what are wealth, possessions, honor, esteem? Nothing! "I regard [all things] as loss, in order that I can gain Christ," cried Saint Paul.[6] And I say the same.

I trust Jesus to value my love, as I value his. He wants only this: "As the Father has loved me, so I have loved you; abide in my love."[7] There is no relationship deeper than love. Two hearts joined in love are as two candles burning so closely together that the flames mingle and become one.

I feel God has so much love to give, but there aren't many ready and able to receive it. Oh yes, they're content to be faithful servants, acquaintances, admirers, but they aren't willing to risk themselves, and so they don't experience, as I have done, God's overwhelming desire to love us with infinite strength and tenderness.

Most of us choose to paddle in the shallows—a bit of

love here, a bit of love there. But I want everything, whole and entire. I want to be open to receive God's love, to burn with it, to spread it and to share it. I have confidence that this is possible, even for me, because I know God has made me just as I am and accepts me in all my human imperfection.

Only love can heal and transform. And God offers it for free. That's why I want to respond by giving myself to God in return—for free, with no conditions whatsoever.

Here are some beautiful verses by a Carmelite saint who truly understood spiritual love. I've meditated on these verses by Saint John of the Cross for years, growing in my understanding of the love God wants to share with us and which alone makes us holy.

Stay with me now as I read these verses to you and with you slowly and prayerfully. If you like, light a candle or play some quiet background music to aid your concentration.

My Beloved is the mountains,
The solitary wooded valleys,
The strange islands,
The roaring torrents,
The whisper of the amorous gales;

The tranquil night
At the approaches of the dawn,
The silent music,
The murmuring solitude,
The supper which revives and enkindles love.

Cease, O thou killing North wind!
Come, O South wind, thou that awakenest love!
Blow through my garden,
And let its odors flow,
And my beloved shall feed among the flowers.

My soul is occupied,
And all my substance in his service;
Now I guard no flock,
Nor have I any other employment:
My sole occupation is love.

If then on common land
I am no longer seen or found,
Say that I am lost;
That being enamored,
I lost myself and yet I was found.[8]

A Call to Love

Each person has his or her own place, own mission. Each one is called to contribute to the whole while striving to be animated by love:

> Love is patient; love is kind; love is not envious or boastful or arrogant or rude. It does not insist on its own way; it is not irritable or resentful; it does not rejoice in wrongdoing, but rejoices in the truth. It bears all things, believes all things, hopes all things, endures all things.[9]

Whether we are contemplatives like Therese (in a convent, an office or on a farm) or active ministers like Dorothy Day (in the parish, the family or the missions), we are called to be love in the heart of the Church.

Everyone has to maintain a balance between prayer and work, though the time given to each may differ. Every one of us is called to be present and committed wherever we are needed, to give our lives selflessly and generously in the situation in which we find ourselves.

Saint and sinner alike, we belong to one another.

> But speaking the truth in love, we must grow up in
> every way into him who is the head, into Christ,
> from whom the whole body, joined and knit
> together by every ligament with which it is
> equipped, as each part is working properly,
> promotes the body's growth in building itself up in
> love.[10]

As we belong to Christ's Body, we are flesh of one other's
flesh and are responsible for one another, not just for
ourselves. Father Timothy Radcliffe, Master of the
Dominican Order, writes of an experience during the civil
war in Rwanda, when only "being love" at the heart of
the Church, being with the poor and marginalized
through common participation in the Eucharist, enabled
people to keep going.

> I think of a day in northern Rwanda, in the war
> zone, before these present troubles. I had visited the
> refugee camp with 30,000 people and had seen
> women trying to feed children who had just given
> up eating because they could not be bothered to live.
> I had visited the hospital run by the sisters, and seen
> ward after ward of children and young people with
> their limbs missing. I remember one child, eight or
> nine, with both his legs blown off, and an arm and
> an eye, and his father sitting by the bed weeping.
> And we went back to the sisters' house and there
> was nothing to say. We could not find a single word.
> But we could celebrate the Eucharist, we could
> remember that Last Supper. It was this, the only
> thing to do, that gave those sisters the courage to
> stay and to belong.
> The deepest truth of our human nature is not
> that we are greedy and selfish but that we hunger

and thirst for God, and in God will find each other.[11]

Sometimes when we look at the newspapers, everything seems hopeless: violence, sexual abuse, poverty, natural disasters, ecological destruction. How is it that our hearts are not touched? Is it not that we feel helpless before the magnitude of the problems that confront us? But love never gives up; it "bears, believes, hopes, endures all things." The sufferers and perpetrators of suffering alike are God's beloved children.

Being love at the heart of the Church means avoiding all condemnation, all sense of superiority. We do not help others by exposing and denouncing their personal sin (though we may do so in relation to a society or group as a whole). Only attentive love, which allows others to feel unthreatened and thus able to disclose themselves in their own time, will foster understanding and compassion. Mercy has been shown to us. Now we must be merciful in our turn. It is because we ourselves have experienced grace and forgiveness that we can diffuse these gifts in a world hungering for healing and salvation.

Julian of Norwich writes much on the mercy and tenderness of God. Like Therese, from the solitude of her anchorhold, she understood well that prayer unites us, and that those who pray do so for and on behalf of others. Prayer and closeness to God also reveal our own frailties, enabling us to grow in self-knowledge and humility; thus compassion grows apace:

> I saw how Christ had compassion on us because of sin. And just as I was before full of pain and compassion because of the passion of Christ, so I was now full of compassion for all my fellow Christians.... And then I saw that every natural

compassion anyone has for a fellow Christian is due to Christ living within.... He also wants us to see that he is our ground, and that his pains and tribulations so far exceed all that we can suffer that it cannot be fully understood. Taking notice of this will prevent us from grumbling and despairing in our own suffering. It makes us see truly that our sin deserves it, but his love excuses us. And in his great courtesy he does away with all our blame and looks upon us with pity and compassion as innocent and beloved children.[12]

Therese, wanting to "be love" in the heart of the Church, finding in love her deepest and most meaningful vocation, did so—not for herself, but on behalf of all. What mattered were not the words she uttered but the disposition to give herself unreservedly to the will of God in her own vocation, entrusting herself entirely.

That was true holiness for her, just as it is for us—and it is within our grasp here and now.

For Reflection

- *Write a prayer in your own words, expressing your desire to love God and to receive God's love.*

- *How do we belong together? What is your own particular place in the Church? The wider community? How can you "be love" in your situation? Share your insights, if you wish, with a friend or coworker.*

- *Think of times when you have felt God present in situations that seemed hopeless or full of despair. Did you have the courage to continue belonging and so go through the darkness into new light and life? How?*

- *What does the symbol of fire say to you? Would you be afraid to ask to be burned up in God's love?*

Closing Prayer

O my God,
I desire to love you and to make you loved.
I desire to accomplish your will perfectly
and to arrive at the degree of glory
you have prepared for me in your kingdom.
In a word, I desire to be holy.
But I know my powerlessness
and ask you, O my God,
to be yourself my holiness.
Jesus told us during his earthly life
"Whatever you ask the Father in my name he will give
   you."
I am certain, then, that you will grant my desires.
I know well, O God,
that the more you give, the more you make us desire.
I feel in my heart immense desires
and I ask you to come and take complete possession of me.
If through weakness I sometimes fall
then may your divine grace purify me once more,
consuming all imperfections
as fire transforms everything into itself.

In the evening of life
I will appear before you with empty hands
for I do not ask you, Lord, to count my works.
I want nothing else apart from you, my Beloved.
In your eyes time is nothing;
a single day is like a thousand years.
You can then, in one instant,

make me ready to appear before you.

In order that my life may be an act of perfect love
I OFFER MYSELF AS A WHOLE BURNT OFFERING
    TO YOUR MERCIFUL LOVE,
begging you to consume me unceasingly.
May the ocean of infinite tenderness contained within you
overflow into my soul
so that I may become a martyr to your love, O Lord.

I desire to renew this offering an infinite number of times
with every heartbeat,
until the shadows depart
and I can tell you eternally of my love, face to
face.—Therese

I ask Lord, that the souls you have entrusted to me may
    experience your love as I have.—Therese

Notes

[1] 1 Corinthians 13:1-3.

[2] "Letter to Marie."

[3] "Letter CLXXXIV," September 17, 1896.

[4] Ida Gorres, *The Nature of Sanctity* (Sheed and Ward, 1932), pp. 62, 61.

[5] *Reminiscences*, p. 70.

[6] Philippians 3:8c.

[7] John 15:9.

[8] Saint John of the Cross, *Verses from the Spiritual Canticle*, trans. D. Lewis.

[9] 1 Corinthians 13:4-7.

[10] Ephesians 4:15, 16.

[11] *The Tablet*, June 18, 1994.

[12] Julian of Norwich, *The Revelations of Divine Love of Julian of Norwich*, trans. James Walsh. Harper, 1961.

DAY SEVEN
A Life of Holiness

Coming Together in the Spirit

On this, the final day of our retreat, Therese is waiting for us in a small prayer room that she has decorated with her own paintings. It is situated just outside the room where she meets daily to talk with the novices. Behind her is a statue of Mary and a vase of flowers—all Therese's favorite wildflowers in a jumble: buttercups, daisies, poppies, mixed grasses and the tiny blue corncockle. The statue, known as Our Lady of the Smile, comes from Therese's family home.

Both Mary and Therese are holding out their hands in a gesture of welcome and friendliness. Therese greets us.

"I've been waiting for you here, praying and thinking about Our Lady, whom I have always found to be a wonderful friend and companion. That's because she is on our side, looking toward God with us. She has traveled along the path towards God as we have to do.

"Mary was only human, yet so holy. And what did she do? Nothing, really, except receive the graces God wanted to give her.

"Mary let herself be used for the world's salvation by consenting to bear Jesus for us. But most of her life was spent in an ordinary family home in an obscure village. When Jesus commended her, it wasn't for her physical motherhood; it was because she heard the word of God and kept it.[1] That relationship is open to us all. Look at this statue and you will see that Mary is smiling and holding out her hands. She is happy to respond to God and invites us to imitate her in her self-surrender.

"Mary wasn't someone who lived constantly with deep insight, miracles or ecstasies. She lived in poverty, following the common way of faith, pondering the mission of her son and her own call to discipleship. When I look at her, I am affirmed in my confidence—confidence in myself and confidence in God, who chooses the weak to confound the strong.[2]

"Merit doesn't consist in doing or giving much, but in receiving, in loving much. Let God give and take what he chooses. Perfection consists in doing his will, and the soul that gives itself totally to him is called by Jesus 'his mother, his sister,' and his whole family. How easy it is to give Jesus pleasure. All one has to do is to love him, not considering oneself, not examining one's faults too closely.[3]

"Don't look at yourself. Look at Jesus. Love him. He will give you all you need if you die to self and receive the gift of a new heart, a new spirit—the spirit of holiness."

Opening Prayer

My God,
you have promised a new heart and a new spirit
to those who love you.
Give me, I pray, a share in the Spirit of Jesus, your
   Son,
and teach me how to live in love.

May I abandon myself to you,

discovering that I can live free from fear,
free from the chains that bind me to myself,
to my past, to my sins,
to wondering what others will say,
because I know I can have confidence in you.

You, Lord, are merciful.
You are kind and compassionate;
you welcome sinners and forgive them completely.
And so I come to you with absolute trust.

My God,
loving you and being loved by you is holiness.
For this gift I hold out my hands.
Grant it to me in Jesus' name. Amen.

RETREAT SESSION SEVEN
Reviewing Our Retreat

Therese Speaks

During these days when we have been together, I have
hoped to foster in you an unshakable confidence in the
merciful love of God and the desire to respond. *It is
enough to realize one's nothingness and give oneself wholly,
like a child, into the arms of the good God.*[4]

This kind of abandonment is only possible if you
believe that you are loved absolutely and
unconditionally. To accept everything as coming to you
from God and to thank God for it is a fundamental
principle of the Christian life and of my way of spiritual
childhood.

To know yourself as a child, cherished and held in the arms of a caring heavenly Father, will help you to overcome all fear and to allow your Father to love you with the tenderness God so longs to pour out upon you. Once you believe this you will be encouraged to act *now*. Turn to God now, pray now—just as you are.

Accepting that life is often hard makes it easier to be courageous in responding to God and finding the strength to overcome your sins and weaknesses. You have to find ways to allow your better self to grow strong—the self hidden beneath all your obsessions, compulsions and lack of freedom.

We all want to be free. But sometimes we try to avoid or forget the truth Jesus revealed to us. Remember when he told the Jews, "...[E]veryone who commits sin is a slave to sin"? "The slave does not have a permanent place in the household; the son has a place there forever. So if the Son makes you free, you will be free indeed."[5] Remaining in the freedom of Jesus requires us to do battle with the forces of sin and selfishness. So let us brandish the sword of the Spirit, my friends, and live by every word we have received from the mouth of God!

And what is it that sustains the warrior? You know the answer. It is love. Listen to these fiery words from the Song of Songs:

> ...[L]ove is strong as death,
>   passion fierce as the grave.
> Its flames are flashes of fire,
>   a raging flame.
> Many waters cannot quench love
>   neither can floods drown it.
> If one offered for love
>   all the wealth of his house,
>   it would be utterly scorned.[6]

It is by meditating on scriptural passages like this one, and especially on the Gospels, that we come to understand what Jesus asks of us.

To live in love is to give without measure,
without demanding any return on earth.
For when you love you don't calculate your profit.

To live in love is to banish all fear
and recollection of past sins and failings,
for everything is obliterated in the divine fire.

To live in love is to possess a great treasure
in an earthen vessel.
My Jesus, my weakness is extreme,
I'm far from being any kind of angel.
But whenever I fall you are there,
holding me, embracing me.
You come to me, giving me grace,
enabling me to live in love.[7]

This, my friends, is the path to holiness for all of us "ordinary people." May our lives draw others to join us on this "little way."

For Reflection

- *Has your picture of God changed as a result of this retreat? If so, how? Share your insights with a friend, if you wish.*

- *What is the difference between being good and being holy? Can you give an example?*

- *Why is holiness a gift to the whole Church? Are you*

convinced that it is possible for you?

- *Write a short prayer of confidence in God, expressing your complete trust.*

Therese Says Good-bye

Do you remember the incident I told you at the beginning of this retreat, when I went off with the basket of dolls' clothes saying, "I choose everything"?

That has been the key to my whole life. Later, when the idea of religious perfection came within my orbit, I realized at once that there's no reaching holiness unless you were prepared to suffer a great deal, to be always on the look out for something higher still, and to forget yourself.

Everyone was free to answer our Lord's invitation by doing a little for him or by doing a lot for him. In fact, he gave us a choice between various kinds of self-sacrifice.

And then, as in babyhood, I found myself crying out, "My God, I choose the whole lot!" There's no point in becoming only a half-saint. I'm not afraid of suffering for you. The only thing I'm afraid of is clinging to my own will. Take it, I want the whole lot, everything whatsoever that is your will for me."[8]

I choose everything. I don't choose only bits and pieces of my life, an episode here or there in which I can see God's hand at work—the day of my First Communion or the days of special celebration and happiness. I choose to see God in absolutely *everything* that happens, joyful or painful, because I am my Father's child, totally dependent on him, gratefully receiving all from him, confident that all he gives me comes from the hand of one who loves me unconditionally.

But God will not force this response from us. We have to desire it and sustain it for a lifetime, and that takes enormous courage and energy. God asks us to trust with our very selves and every aspect of our lives, whatever comes our way.

This is what I have had to do. It's true that I had a good home and a happy childhood, but when I entered Carmel my days of immaturity had to come to an end. I had to learn a new gospel, based on spiritual childhood, and make an adult commitment to it.

Mine were the sorrows, struggles and joys that make up most lives in various degrees. The small daily choices that fell to me I made the matter for holiness, whereas many people overlook them or think of them as worthless.

Sustaining and growing in an attitude of gospel childlikeness over the years meant total dependence on God, choosing every event as coming as a gift, refusing nothing, finding hints of divinity everywhere, wanting only to please and thank God and return love for love. That, as you know, is not child's play.

One life of love, trust and confidence affects everyone else in the world in some mysterious way, for love is never wasted, even when hidden behind walls. As Scripture says, God "will not overlook your work and the love that you showed for his sake."[9]

Do you want to share these insights? Do you want to trust God enough to let yourself be carried, loved, with all the tenderness and compassion a mother feels for her own child? Do you want friendship with and likeness to Jesus?

If you want these things, why hold back? Because you are not worthy? Not good enough? Not as "holy" as I am? Because you have a sinful past and fail over and over again?

All you have to do is to open your hands and heart and receive holiness with all the confidence and trust of a little child. Remember: It's love I ask for, love is all the skill I have.

Notes

[1] See Luke 11:27-28.
[2] See 1 Corinthians 1:27.
[3] "Letter CXXI," July 6, 1893.
[4] "Letter CCIII," May 9, 1897.
[5] John 8:35a-36.
[6] Song of Songs 8:6b-7.
[7] *Poems*, adapted.
[8] *Autobiography*, Chapter IV.
[9] Hebrews 6:10b.

Deepening Your Acquaintance

Therese's Writings

The translations of Therese's *Letter to Marie* and *Act of Oblation* have been made specially for this volume by Margaret Needham, O.D.C.

Autobiography, trans. R. Knox. Fontana, 1958.

Collected Letters, trans. F. Sheed. Sheed & Ward, 1949.

Story of a Soul, trans. R. Knox. Collins, 1958.

Poems, trans. Carmelites of Santa Clara. Burns & Oates, 1925.

Books About Therese

Carmelite Sisters. *Following St. Therese*. Birline, 1984.

Gaucher, Guy. *The Passion of St. Therese*. St. Paul, 1987.

_____. *The Spiritual Journey of St. Therese*. DLT, 1987.

Johnson, William. *Silent Music*. Collins, 1974.

Lafrance, Jean. *My Vocation is Love*. St. Paul, 1990.

Sullivan J., ed. *Experiencing St. Therese Today*. Institute of Carmelite Studies, 1990.

Von Balthasar, H. V. *Therese of Lisieux*. Sheed & Ward, 1953.

Audiocassettes

Dorgan, Margaret. *Guidance in Prayer From Three Women Mystics: Julian of Norwich, Teresa of Avila, Therese of Lisieux*. Credence Cassettes. Seven audiocassettes with bibliography.

_____. *Therese of Lisieux*. Credence Cassettes. Single audiocassette.